CREATING A PERENNIAL GARDEN

IN THE MIDWEST

JOAN SEVERA

Trails Media Group, Inc.
Black Earth, Wisconsin

Library of Congress Catalog Card Number: 99-71305
ISBN: 0-915024-73-X

Editor: Stan Stoga
Designer: Kathie Campbell

Printed in China by Everbest Printing Co.,Ltd.
06 05 04 03 02   6 5 4 3

Photo credits: All photos by Joan Severa except where noted.

Trails Books, a division of Trails Media Group, Inc.
P.O. Box 317 • Black Earth, WI 53515
(800) 236-8088   email: info@wistrails.com
www.trailsbooks.com

This book must be dedicated to my most loyal supporter, my husband, Jim.
Though I am sure he hasn't a clue why I spend so much of my life
either gardening or writing about it, he has been able not only to put up
with all the disruption but to admire the results.

While I have spent this year meeting deadlines, rereading, revising endlessly,
and laboring over a complicated index, his patience has meant a lot to me.

Thanks, Jim, and sorry for all the toasted-cheese sandwiches.

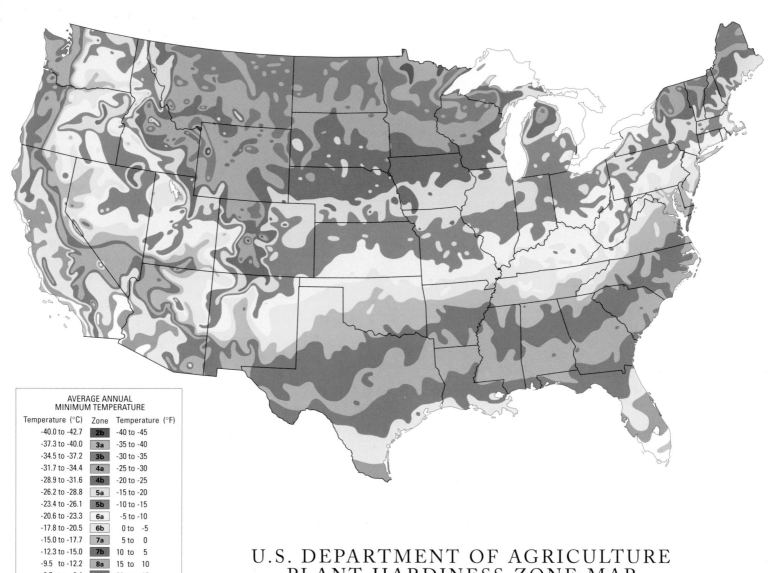

AVERAGE ANNUAL
MINIMUM TEMPERATURE

Temperature (°C)	Zone	Temperature (°F)
-40.0 to -42.7	2b	-40 to -45
-37.3 to -40.0	3a	-35 to -40
-34.5 to -37.2	3b	-30 to -35
-31.7 to -34.4	4a	-25 to -30
-28.9 to -31.6	4b	-20 to -25
-26.2 to -28.8	5a	-15 to -20
-23.4 to -26.1	5b	-10 to -15
-20.6 to -23.3	6a	-5 to -10
-17.8 to -20.5	6b	0 to -5
-15.0 to -17.7	7a	5 to 0
-12.3 to -15.0	7b	10 to 5
-9.5 to -12.2	8a	15 to 10
-6.7 to -9.4	8b	20 to 15
-3.9 to -6.6	9a	25 to 20
-1.2 to -3.8	9b	30 to 25
1.6 to -1.1	10a	35 to 30
4.4 to 1.7	10b	40 to 35

U.S. DEPARTMENT OF AGRICULTURE
PLANT HARDINESS ZONE MAP

Contents

CONTENTS

Introduction

If lawn mowing feels like copying the same sentence over and over, gardening is like

writing out new ones, an infinitely variable process of invention and discovery.

Michael Pollan, *Second Nature*, Dell Publishing, 1991

THIS BOOK IS SINCERELY meant to help the home gardener in the upper north temperate zone who attempts, without a staff of gardeners or the backup of a nursery on the premises, to keep a perennial garden attractive all season long. This means, of course, that spring bulbs are followed by early, mid, and then late perennials, and that plants which appear at the same time are mutually complementary in leaf, height, and blossom. No mean trick!

It can take a lifetime to work out all the variables for a reliable underplanting this far north, where winter protection adds its uncertainty, especially when every stage of planning and work are done by one person. You might say I am intensely interested in keeping the labor within the capacities of a single person; I do all of my gardening alone.

My idea with this book is to share my personal experiences in creating gardens and growing perennials under these conditions, and to show that good planning can minimize the labor; that once established, a perennial garden that is rich in compatible plants and well mulched does not have to be that labor intensive.

My garden is in a partly wooded suburban lot in USDA Zone 4, give or take a little; some winters are warmer, some as cold as Zone 3. Zone 4 temperatures can get as low as -20 degrees; Zone 3, as low as -30. Some years we have a lot of snow, some years very little.

Like most home gardeners, I have grown—and therefore can talk about—only a modest selection from the thousands of perennials available. The plants I include in this book are my favorites: those that have responded best to tough conditions and, as a result, are in my opinion most worth cultivating.

As a graduate of the Master Gardener series in Wisconsin, I have been working for many years, both hands-on and in lectures, to help spread basic good gardening techniques. I hear the same questions at every lecture: "How do I start a new garden?" "Where should I put it?" "What should I plant?" "Why doesn't my garden look nice any more?" "What's a good fertilizer?" "What will grow in that bare patch under the trees?" and "What can I plant that will bloom all summer?" I hate this last question—the questioner usually means one variety of plant that will stay in bloom all year. A non-creative approach, to say the least.

I have noticed what seems to be a dual, mutually contradictory view of gardening held by the complete novice: on the one hand is the idea that a small hole in the lawn, just large enough to hold the roots or the bulb, is an okay way to start a plant growing. On the other hand is the vague impression that, to be gardeners, people have to know much more than they really want to know. Just hearing about mulching, winter protection, pruning, or any of the gentle tasks that keep gardeners busy, is enough to turn them off.

I feel a personal obligation to help demystify these processes, though I like to make clear that a certain amount of basic preparation (work!) is absolutely necessary for good results. It isn't that difficult. Everything can be simplified.

I find that even experienced gardeners are grateful for step-by-step instructions, the more basic and often repeated, the better. Gardeners, even beginning ones, are not afraid of work, just afraid of making mistakes—of killing good plants after all their efforts. Strangely enough, when I assure beginners that no amount of education saves even the best gardeners from making mistakes and losing plants, they begin to believe they can be gardeners too.

I know how intimidating it is to feel we need to know everything before even beginning. But that is such a self-defeating attitude! I believe we can simplify: use common sense, get as much basic information as possible, and then just go ahead, learning on the way.

For years I hesitated over writing this book. Should I dare? I am not a trained horticulturist, plant propagator, or ecologist; I am no more than a self-taught back yard gardener. But, I reasoned, an experienced one, and one with an interesting garden. Also one who has a hatful of inexpensive, simple tricks to improve soil and get things to grow.

Before any big writing project, whether a grant proposal or a book, my first step has always been to form a clear, brief statement of purpose. What is mine? I would say it is to make the whole process of gardening accessible to everyone. Yes, everyone! I would like the whole world to have the same kind of joy I have had through working in my garden.

Gardening wisdom takes years of practice to develop, and I've had plenty of time. Time, of course, also promotes the growth of idiosyncrasies. So you will hear a lot of my notions in this book, mostly aimed at simplifying the work. I am not apologizing for them. Whenever I hear any of the world's most famous gardeners lecture, or read one of their books, I come across highly opinionated statements. Even down-home gardeners of my acquaintance can be opinionated. I don't agree with a lot of their opinions but am glad they express them. I think different methods work for different people; a degree of magic is involved in gardening, and rituals carried out by believers are often quite effective. All good gardeners have pet theories! You may ignore those of mine that don't appeal to you, and please feel free to develop some of your own.

No two gardeners have the same drive or vision, let alone the same conditions. I try to give people the simplest ways to handle perennials given our conditions. Mostly, my method consists of telling them why and how I did the job and discussing the results I achieved. I am positive that this process will be encouraging and helpful to you, no matter what your gardening style or preferences.

I would like to have you regard this book as you would a demonstration by a watercolorist: enjoy the pictures, compare the way the artist sees and does things to the way you do, possibly discover more about your own vision, pick up any techniques you might be able to use, learn about some different materials, perhaps get a few new angles, then go out and paint your own picture.

How My Garden Began

Gardening is complex because it combines aesthetic judgements and practical decisions with

the science of craftmanship in a kaleidoscope of variables. A poet is limited to the dictionary,

a sculptor starts with a block of stone, but a gardener starts with a plot that is frozen one day

and flooded the next, here in sun and there in shadow, teased by the wind

and tantalized by drought, plagued by insects, toyed with by birds, mined by moles.

Hugh Johnson, *Principles of Gardening—The Practice of the Gardener's Art*
Simon & Schuster, 1996 Edition

HATEVER YOUR CIRCUMSTANCES, they can't be much worse than what I faced when I began my garden. In 1976 I came to my current home, a scalped slope of subsoil and builder's fill, edged with huge, half-dead European honeysuckle bushes, buckthorn, wild cherry, woodbine, and wild grape vines, all overshadowed by enormous trees. The poor, scanty lawn was three years old.

The soil in this lawn is that heavy clay so often associated with glaciated areas, the kind that has small, medium-sized, and large rocks sunk in it like nuts in chocolate—hard to dig, hard to clear, and short on organic material. Other typical soils in the upper Midwest include vast sandy prairies, nearly bare continental shelf, wetland, and forest loam. You are as likely to have any of these other soil conditions as to share mine. Bear with me as I deal with the work it took to make my soil better, and I think you'll discover that we have a lot in common.

Excess Trees and Undergrowth

My first troubles, as I intimated above, were with the many things already growing on the property. In the front yard, the locust tree, *Robinia pseudoacacia*, was fairly small when we first arrived, and still attractive in that feathery way locusts have. Eventually it grew awfully large, and I was forever climbing up and cutting out watersprouts and branches growing every which way into the center of the tree. It became a messy tree, dropping twigs along with small, plentiful leaves into the downspouts after it grew tall enough. Thin, weak branches were forever growing downward and having to be taken off at the main limb. Knuckles of gnarly root were popping up farther and farther from the trunk, where sprouts formed after every rain. I was not a bit sorry when the tree split in a wind storm and had to be taken out.

Several other excess trees lived in my space for a short while after I came on the scene. Three Norway maples, *Acer platanoides*, had been planted much too close to each other along the east border. Two we had removed, and the other we pruned to twenty feet above the ground. I wish we had taken it out as well. Its shallow roots rob the soil of nutrients and moisture, and make gardening on that side of the driveway difficult. We don't need the shade on our east side, as the trees in the neighbor's yard provide more shade than I like now that they're grown. The maple seeds sailing down in summer take root with alarming fecundity and are hard to pull up. The maple's one saving grace is its beautiful yellow fall color, although when the huge leaves come down all at once that doesn't seem such a bonus either.

Three spruce trees of doubtful lineage had been planted in the obligatory triangle at the foot of the driveway. Two of these, about three feet tall (with enormous rootballs!) I dug and transported in my garden cart to other places in the yard, where they still thrive in part shade. The other, the bluest, became infested with spruce gall, and we eventually lost it.

In the area thus freed I started a rather large, roughly triangular garden at the foot of the sloping driveway for plants requiring more sun. I was warned that the runoff from the drive would wash out any garden there. The driveway slopes down into this bed, so I created a stone-lined "brook" at the driveway's lowest point to carry runoff through the bed to the bottom border, which was dug into a shallow trench to catch the overflow. Shade from the neighbor's house covers the area most of the morning, and from our house most of the afternoon, but the open sky above is enough for all but the most demanding plants, even some shrub roses. Once the soil was amended, the garden was on its way. I believe the greatest satisfactions in gardening come from rescuing trouble spots and turning them into assets!

The overgrown European honeysuckle bushes, *Lonicera tatarica*, not only lined the edges of my lawn when I first came to the property, but filled the next-door woodlot. They were mostly dead and partly horizontal, those on my lawn lying toward the house, taking up about ten feet of border space. While they had shallow roots so that I was able to pry the rootstocks out of the ground after I cut back the trunks, they were so plentiful and so heavy that it was two or three years before I had them all out. My difficulty was compounded by intertwining grapevines, probably fifty years old, climbing up through the bushes and high into the wild cherries, hickories, and oaks. I removed the honeysuckle lying over the lawn early on, but the whole tangle didn't come down fully until about 1995, when the new neighborhood went in and bulldozers pushed through for the utilities next to our lot. The consequent loss of the wild-seeded apple trees and the cool breath of woodsy shade was ameliorated greatly by the increase of softly filtered afternoon sunlight for the east border.

Weed Trees

An even worse problem was caused by the *Rhamnus cathartica*, the common buckthorn, which was thriving in the understory. Each year as the plentiful crop of black berries drops to the ground, a new host of tiny seedling trees has been coming up. Each can be pulled up easily, but in their thousands they were almost too much to contemplate. Full-grown trees survived, complete with berries and a crop of saplings, until 1997, when we finally cleared the woodlot.

Wild black cherry trees, *Prunus serotina*, are almost as bad at seeding as buckthorn, and although these trees are probably not as much of a problem—and some of them have grown to forty feet in my borders—they are not very healthy, and I removed many of the little ones.

PHOTOGRAPHY BY TOM COTTINGTON

I hate to take them all out, however. The first year we were here I discovered a wonderful recipe. A few quarts of the tart black cherries make a delicious cherry bounce with the addition of sugar and brandy. After aging quietly for a month or two, the mixture is decanted into dark glass bottles. Taken in small cordial glasses, the beverage warmed our evenings for several years.

Beautiful Shade Lost

When we first moved to the property, the entire backyard was an oak woods with very little light. Huge oak trees reached branches to the patio doors and down to the ground in many places. Unfortunately, the sloping lot had been developed by an insensitive crew, who piled soil three or four feet high around four of the oaks closest to the house, thereby guaranteeing that they would die. After about twelve years they yellowed, shriveled, and died, all in one summer,

The north slope, behind the old open deck, had been heavily shaded by tall oaks and had many small oak saplings. Grass was thin and weak, and the saplings were constantly being clipped by the mower. One of the earliest improvements was to lay a large area of shredded bark around all these trees.

and had to be cut down. It was heartbreaking. If ever you have the option available, never allow even one foot of soil to be applied around an oak from its trunk all the way out to the drip line. Oaks have breather roots, and without enough oxygen they will absolutely die, though it takes about ten years or so. Undisturbed they might live two or three hundred years.

A *Populus alba*, which we called a big-leaf aspen, finally had to be removed in 1996 after one of its twenty-foot branches, thick as your thigh, came crashing down—not during a storm but on a still day—narrowly missing our lawn-mowing friend and gouging deep holes in the turf. This tall tree had given the high shade that protected tender perennials and spoken its clattering, rustling talk in the slightest breeze. I miss the sound. The fact that it still sends up tough switches from its roots, some of them fifty feet from the old trunk, is an unpleasant side effect that I hope disappears in time.

Those were losses I mourned. But now I have more light, and the garden saga can take a new tangent and continue on into further beauty. More plants will grow and bloom here. There is room for more small trees.

Do you know, I think gardening teaches one to get on with life, no matter what the losses, and to make the best of it. It's the only life we have, after all.

Getting Energized

I was not discouraged when I first saw this site. Far from it. Having lived in a developer's desert in a prefab home, this wooded lot seemed like heaven to me, and all I saw were the possibilities. Former owners had been trying desperately (and unsuccessfully) to make it into a suburban turf lawn for three years. Anyone could see this wasn't working, and the results were bare and ugly. (Well, they hadn't had much time.) Yet I realized early on that this failure gave me a real advantage: I had a clear slate upon which I could write my own version of paradise. I began immediately to make gardens. I wanted gardens. I needed gardens. I knew a little about shade plants and ground covers. I had a legacy of hand-me-down daylilies and hostas. Native ferns and wild flowers grew all around in the woods. I dreamed of drifts of textured green in the shady back, billows of color in the slightly sunnier front, and naturalized bluebells and daffodils.

A Fumbling Start

I did some good, basic things, like correcting drainage in the worst areas, and tearing out the honeysuckle bushes and unwanted trees, but in other ways I also made every wrong start possible. I did almost no soil amendment (I called it "dirt" then). I underestimated the impermeable nature of the basic clay subsoil and put things in inadequate holes, which filled up with water. I made gardens that were too small, and I couldn't keep the grass out of them. I made gardens that were too big, and I didn't make paths in them. I planted everything I was given, including some invasive beauties such as *Lysimachia clethroides* (gooseneck loosestrife), which should be placed only where it has a clear run and cannot encroach upon any garden plants. I didn't mulch, except once with heavy gravel over plastic, which became a weedy disaster in six months. I tossed enormous quantities of leaves into waste corners and left them to rot, never thinking of using them. I lost many plants I could have saved, but whose requirements I didn't know, either through carelessness or ignorance.

I had successes, too, of course, because for any given situation there is a plant that actually likes it. Mostly, this success was accidental.

Moving native plants from nearby woodlots just ahead

of the bulldozers was one of my more successful experiments. Where my soil had been left in its original state near the sides and back of the lawn, these native plants loved the dryness and shade under the tall trees; it was home turf. *Adiantum pedatum*, the native maidenhair fern, has been the best example, forming huge billows at woodsy edges and along paths. When I moved such plants into the fill dirt around the house, however, they withered and died. The fill used to level the soil around houses such as mine comes from the excavation of the basement, well below the soil line, down into the clay subsoil. It is barren of organic material and soil microorganisms, so although it is loaded with minerals, plants have no access to them. These areas need to be heavily amended with manure, compost, peat, bark, garbage, garden waste, or anything else organic, then tilled and left to rest over a winter. This painful lesson took a few years to sink in for me; I recommend that you take it to heart.

The Magic of Wood Chips

Almost through accident, I learned what decomposing wood chips and bark can do for poor soil. There were several areas of sapling oak trees in the yard, which were getting scraped and wounded by the lawnmower, and from a local supplier of railroad ties I had rough bark hauled in (and I mean rough—it contained strips of wide bark three feet long and big chips and splinters of wood), and I had it laid down almost a foot thick in broad beds, over layers of soaked newspapers, around groups of the young trees. Then, because I was busy with other areas, I left those patches alone for a year or two. They looked serene and graceful enough in their bark covering, and I didn't mind the lack of green growth.

In three years those bark beds were like native woodlot, standing thick with volunteer wild plants and even shrubs. Birds and squirrels had planted *Sambucus nigra*, the native

By the time the old deck was replaced with a screened porch, the bark beds had been filled full of shade-loving plants. Every spring these beds expand a little more, as I cut back sod and add to the borders. Since this photograph was taken, a new two-foot border of pulmonarias sparkles around the long side to the left.

This bed is a testimonial to my favorite garden imperatives: to keep edges fluid, to prune trees high and surround them with a substantial footing of mixed, companionable plantings, and to keep everything lush and healthy with bark and manure.

elderberry, and *Cornus sericea*, the red-twig dogwood bushes. Voles had brought *Polygonatum commutatum*, Solomon's seal; *Uvularia grandiflora*, bellwort; *Aquilegia canadensis*, columbine; the native, fast-spreading *Chelidonium* (celandine), or wood poppy; three or four varieties of violets; and *Arisaema triphyllum*, jack-in-the-pulpit. I soon found I could insinuate cultivated and other wild plants beautifully into this mix simply by digging out something I didn't want and putting in something more appropriate.

After a while, the soil was improved very deeply, far below the original newspaper and bark. I could hardly believe it! Bark and manure have been added in alternating years ever since, but I have never done anything else to improve the soil in those bark beds except for amendments in the planting holes of some choice specimens. These are now among the loveliest spots in the garden, containing many healthy shade plants.

The top dressing I add approximately every other year goes on all my garden beds and consists of an inch or two of either finely shredded bark or manure. I add it in early June, as a rule, when everything is up but there is not too much leafage. This gives me the chance to pull the material a few inches away from all the stems, because it's best to have that area clear of debris to give slugs, insects, and molds less of a chance. You will find several strong reminders in this book about bark mulches: unless they are fully decomposed at the time you apply them, it is necessary to add nitrogen-rich fertilizer under the mulch.

This treatment will do good things even if it is the only thing you do to the soil. Microorganisms by the multimillions breed in the decomposing organic material—and we do not even know all the delicate interactions they cause when added to soil, or how it happens. It is known that organic additives encourage beneficial worms and insects, provide nutrients, protect plants from diseases, strengthen growth, and promote healthy conditions. After all, nature has been doing it this way forever.

Granted, it's possible that elements in some loads of composted manure or plant material are less than ideal: for instance, the manure of beef cattle given steroids might contain residues of those drugs. I think the best way to combat this possibility is the way I choose my own food: I do not rely on a steady diet of one or two types of food, but alternate among the different kinds, sticking to pure organics as much as possible.

Inspiration

Visiting public and private gardens has always been my most inspiring activity. I venture to say that I have never made such a visit without bringing home at least one new thought, whether of a plant, a combination of plants, or of some cultural revelation.

The bonus in garden visiting is that one invariably discovers new friends. Gardening is like that. Friends who share one's little pleasures and great excitements are not that plentiful in life as a whole, but in gardening they abound.

I have always been a reader, and garden magazines and books have filled my bookshelves the way leaves filled the corners of my lawn. Books might be the most inspirational activity of all for a gardener. I read everything pertaining to gardens, cover to cover. I began to learn things about good culture from articles in the magazines, usually at least one salient fact per issue. I picked up a thousand little gems of positive value: lavender needs sharp drainage, so set it in sand; dianthus, too, will die without very good drainage; don't touch gas plant leaves, they contain a photosensitive irritant; daffodils, unlike tulip and crocus bulbs, are not supposed to be interesting to squirrels, rabbits, or deer.

Gradually, more and more of these individual facts accrued into a small lump of solid knowledge; just enough for me to begin to realize how little I knew, and how little was actually being written about gardening vicissitudes in the north temperate zone.

In my early days of gardening, I searched always for more specific written information for this zone, but though I found many bits of good stuff, I could never find a book that dealt with both the creative search for hardy plants and the special issues of growing them under our cold-climate conditions. I am thankful that writers are now addressing our area so that you will soon be able to find books on every specialty for our northern climate.

Finding New Books

It wasn't until 1998 that someone finally published a thorough, all-inclusive reference work about our special conditions, which can be of enormous help to all of us. *Growing Perennials in Cold Climates* by Mike Heger and John Whitman deals with fifty perennial groups and more than "1,700 Varieties Proved to Thrive in Cold Climates" — all in alphabetical order. The contents range from ratings and commercial sources for hard-to-find plants to information on selecting, planting, cutting, drying, companion planting, and all the issues of culture and disease control. There are excellent photographs of individual plants in blossom. This book is precious beyond my ability to describe it. No perennial gardener should be without it.

The Well-Tended Garden by Tracy DiSabato-Aust obviously deals with the care of the garden. It is divided into three parts: basic planting and maintenance, pruning techniques, and an alphabetically arranged encyclopedia of perennials. Writing in Ohio, this author has nearly the same deadly winter conditions we have, and most of the plants about which she writes can be grown here. The author is a garden designer who personally selects plants and creates gardens for clients and draws upon a staff for installation. This book should be kept at hand the entire working season, for it is filled with priceless professional advice.

A new book, *Daffodils for American Gardens* by Brent and Becky Heath, is another for which I am grateful. Even if you have never been a daffodil enthusiast, this astonishingly complete reference will have you eager to get started. It is illustrated with many gorgeous photographs of individual varieties, companion plantings, and great gardens. It is inclusive, I believe, of every known type, and it describes daffodils for every possible condition. Along with this, you find hints of the Heaths' personalities, such as this: "Try to get others interested in bulbs." I like their spirit. I am doing just that when I tell you to keep this book in hand when planning every new garden bed, so that daffodils will be included everywhere.

Another good American book with excellent information for northern gardeners is *A Year at North Hill* by Wayne Winterrowd and Joe Eck, written in chilly Vermont. Because of special environmental factors, the authors grow some marginally hardy perennials that probably wouldn't survive here, but they also offer you much in-depth information about plants that are appropriate to our area. All this, along with engaging writing and great photographs. A great winter read.

Wisconsin's own Marlyn Sachtjen has given us all a mountain of inspiration and advice in her chatty *Marlyn's Garden*, which details the creation of her six-acre site in southern Wisconsin with plants tailored to this climate, most grown by her from seed. Marlyn's garden includes a wild prairie and an arboretum of hardy trees and shrubs, as well as huge drifts of bulb plants and hardy perennials, rich and colorful all year long. The garden itself is a famous teaching place and meeting place for gardeners, and a model for local ecologists.

Certainly many other books exist that are helpful. Even those written to glorify foreign gardens may provide a glimpse of a plant combination that will work here or may give you a new plant to consider. Although books about gardens in milder countries can be awfully misleading, there is some meat to be derived from most of them.

The Great English Books

We are accustomed to looking to England for our garden books. The English climate has given rise to a race of dedicated, earnest gardeners, and from among them have risen many world-famous garden writers. It is now the custom for such books to be inclusive of U.S. zonal and cultural information, so these do help with the selection of plants for our area. I recommend owning them all, of course. Any book that speaks of gardens is good winter reading, and any good writing is good for the soul. The best of these books, garden-wise, are those that should be kept at one's elbow all winter long, along with special catalogs, just to get the reader through the doldrums and inspire yet another glorious spring. Even if these great books do talk about some plants that will not grow here, they nevertheless inspire us to stretch the envelope and create good micro-environmental situations for less hardy beauties.

I have chosen not to include either a bibliography or a lengthy list of books, and having mentioned the few new American books that have direct bearing on our conditions, I limit myself to one of my favorite English gardeners and her writings.

Beth Chatto's *The Green Tapestry* is the most inspiring garden book of any I have ever read. Unfortunately, this book is out of print. I don't know how to explain why this book is so important to me, but this author's feeling for plants comes across very clearly in her writings, along with her love for putting them together in mutually enhancing combinations. It is the combinations that draw me. This kind of communication transcends climatic boundaries. Chatto's information is founded on her understanding of the provenance of the plants she grows and their special requirements. She writes to the gardener in us, wherever we are.

Three of her earlier books, Beth Chatto's *Garden Jour-*

nal, *The Dry Garden*, and *The Damp Garden*, have recently been reprinted by Sagapress, and I recommend them highly, with the caveat that you may be overwhelmed by the sheer volume of plant material that can be grown in the more lenient English climate, and also by the manner in which even our familiar plants respond to that climate. We can't hope for such results, obviously. Yet I say that is not important; Chatto's books are much more than catalogs of plants, they are catechisms of planting. You cannot help but learn from them.

Specialty Catalogs

You will find a lot of good information nowadays in the better catalogs from growers, where new things are introduced every year. It seems to me that the number of good nurseries and good catalogs is increasing annually. The more good gardeners you meet, the more catalogs you will hear of. Garden catalog writers of today are learning to feel for the inexperienced gardener to an increasing degree, so that you can learn almost everything you need to know if you read very carefully about each plant you wish to purchase. It will not all be in one catalog, so reading every one you can get your hands on will absolutely increase your level of competence.

Beginning
Your Own Garden

No two gardens are the same. No two days are the same in one garden.

And yet on this flapping canvas an amateur, often without previous experience,

and holding the instruction book in one hand, tries to daub a vision of a better world . . .

Hugh Johnson, *Principles of Gardening—The Practice of the Gardener's Art*
Simon and Schuster, 1996 Edition

EFORE PLANNING your garden, you may need to work a bit on your notions about this geographical location. Gardening in the Midwest is not a liability but a marvelous opportunity. This is a miraculous area for gardens! The freezing cold and snow of the long winters work like nothing else in nature to help modify heavy soils and enrich poor ones, just through the constant freeze-thaw, the heaving and settling, and the aeration that takes place. The leaves that fall are nature's bounty for mulching and protecting tender plants. Some of the most beautiful plants ever grown thrive in this environment. Nothing in the world compares with a northern spring spangled with spring-flowering bulbs you have set in yourself, unless it is a brisk fall day on the cusp of a long winter of rest, with masses of fall asters to complement autumn leaves.

These are boom days for the home gardener. Boom days for the nurseries and breeders, also, as it becomes more and more easy to find suppliers in an ever-increasing market. Garden tours take place annually in every community. Gardens are constantly being featured on TV and in the Sunday supplements in newspapers. Everyone's neighbors have gardens set into their lawns. Garden centers offer fresh, viable plants all summer long, no longer dwindling to a few dried-up specimens by Memorial Day as was common just a few years ago. There are exponentially doubled numbers of cultivars of some of the more popular perennials, and whole societies of devotees for each species. Garden catalogs are not only multiplying, but vying with one another in content, attractiveness, and charm. Prices, overall, are coming down. We are told that the quantity and quality of new plant resources is just beginning to take off. It is impossible to escape being touched by the lure of gardening these days, and easier than ever to become an educated gardener.

Opposite: All of these plants, and more, were removed and set in tubs to await the arrival of mixed soil. Unfortunately, it was an unusually wet spring, and the wait was long. A few plants were lost before I could get them into the new bed.

Learning Makes the Garden Grow

You will be able to make gardens after reading these books. They will grow, and you will make better gardens next year, and still better gardens over the coming years as you learn more. You will never stop learning, so your garden will never stop evolving. That's the way it should be. Learn from your garden! Learn from books, gardeners' organizations, public gardens, and especially the newly proliferating gardening courses and seminars. Take the Master Gardener Series if there is one in your area. Join the Hardy Plant Society and meet other gardeners.

Best Tips from an Old Gardener

For the benefit of both your garden and your physical stamina, I give you my first, and most heartfelt, piece of advice: start small. Not small in terms of size, necessarily, but in scope. Do one area at a time, and give yourself at least a season to develop this area before going on to the next. If you work outside the home and have limited time to garden, keep this area to a manageable size and use your very favorite plants.

Here is another piece of good advice, which does not always occur to me in time to save me from a lot of work: a garden should be made large enough in the first place to be effective for its purpose. If it is a border, it must show distinctively from a distance. If it is a small setting for alpines, it will look best if it is framed and spaced out to give the effect of a mountain field in miniature. If it is a "woodland" around a tree or shrub, it should not ring the trunk in a tight circle but loop out nearly to the drip line, at least on one axis.

This tip extends to visualizing the size of your plants. It is really, really important to back off from a new garden site and try to envision it with mature plants growing to see whether you have good aesthetic balance. Choosing lots of

Top: This photograph is still exciting to me because of the wonderful plant combinations, but it shows clearly that I did not plan carefully enough when I first built the berm. I built it well enough, but I laid it out in an unimaginative lozenge-shape and set it straight with the back edge of the lawn. It needed to be higher, and it needed to extend to the right in a triangular form to fill the lawn corner more proportionately.

Bottom: The new outline was cut in a trench on one end of the berm, bringing it out into a rounded, somewhat heart-shaped triangle. Two yards of mixed soil were ordered to raise the right center at least two feet higher, with levels extending to the foreground. Large rocks were hauled over from other areas for use in the new, raised end of the berm.

small plants, with no size differences, gives you a dull garden, no matter how individually charming the plants may be. A garden of all medium-sized plants, without some taller plants for relief, does the same. Even a grove of trees becomes more interesting with variations in height.

Design Principles Work

A gardener who might be totally unaware of the principles involved may still be subliminally pleased by a design that follows certain basic proportions and ideas, and may sense something lacking when these basics have not been followed. While "laws" of proportion guide artists and architects, we need not worry too much about precision in our own gardens. I believe you can learn to sense good design through observation.

Merely making a garden (and its plants) large enough in proportion to house, background trees, and surrounding lawn fulfills one of the main principles. After that, a sort of unofficial rule of thirds can be kept in mind: place taller accent plants off center, for instance, about a third of the length of the garden. Use a pyramidal structure when you arrange plants, with your tallest plant forming the apex of a triangle, and the heights of accompanying plants descending approximately by thirds. These triangles may interlock at their bases, infinitely, for continued interest in a long border. Try for a natural, uncontrived appearance. You may be surprised at the professional-looking results you can obtain.

A small round or square garden with one big plant in the middle, bracketed or surrounded evenly with matching plants, needs a rigid, formal setting to come off well. It is not a subject for middle-of-the-lawn placement. Neither is a little patch with tiny plants. Either will be lost and make the lawn look patchy. Better, for an informal look, is a larger and longer shape to your planting area, with one large feature plant about two-thirds of the way along, a few strong shapes along the center or back in an irregular placement, and medium and smaller specimens tucked into the edges.

To make small spaces seem larger, there are tricks of the eye that work wonders. Paths that lead the eye off into a vista or that curve around behind tall screening plants here and there give the illusion of secret hidden places and of a lot more space. Sometimes one has to wait a year or so, while plants grow, for such ideas to suggest themselves. But do not be put off by having a small, circumscribed plot of land to work with. Some of the most fascinating gardens I've ever

seen began as small, plain backyards. Oddly, closing in some garden "rooms" and laying out paths, although using up space, seem to add to it!

Some proportions are recommended more for physical than for artistic reasons: a strip for a foundation planting around your house, for instance, needs to be at least six feet

Top: About three weeks after the new outline was cut, topsoil mixed with sand and manure was delivered for the newly shaped berm. The soil was piled, the rocks were set, and the plants were put in on the same day. The berm was gently watered and mulched for the best recovery possible. While the berm planting looks new and tentative again, I am pleased. The size and shape now fits the northeast rear corner much more comfortably, and the new rock placement gives good footing for tending the bed.

Bottom: The loss of a tall big-leaf aspen tree in the backyard put the new shady berm in a difficult situation, with hot sun for two hours or so every noon. I needed a new tree, not too large, to put west of the berm to shade it in the afternoon and to add its own beauty. I selected *Ilex verticillata*, winterberry, and set it on a small berm, separated from the larger one by a grass path.

This ilex is one of those fruiting trees needing a male of the same species to fertilize it in blossom time; otherwise it will not have berries. I planted the little male tree about twenty feet away, where it will help to shade the east border plants.

As the locust tree grew, it shaded the front yard more and more heavily. Neighboring trees had not yet grown enough to shut out the morning sun, and this small patch at the top of the driveway was home to a group of sun-loving plants: the yellow evening primrose, or sundrop, an unnamed pink coral bell, and *Hemerocallis* 'Gala Greetings'. I always thoroughly enjoyed the pinks and yellows together, complete with the touches of orange in the daylilies, despite what some famous garden colorists have to say on the subject.

My garden is so full of chance seedlings and other gifts that I have learned to see the beauty in many a surprising combination.

deep so that the chief plants may be set out three feet from the house, well out of the dry area under the eaves, while still presenting a clear area along their feet for a front border of annuals and smaller plants. Borders along lawn edges need to be nearly as deep, for good effect. These will usually be more beautiful if they are deeper than six feet in important places, such as around trees and shrubs, and somewhat shallower where special treasures are planted for up-close viewing.

Do It Your Way but Don't Be Inflexible

I repeat this admonition frequently: do not be put off by thinking that you do not know "the right way" to do everything. It almost goes without saying that if a thousand gardeners were each given identical plots of land, a thousand very different gardens would be developed. You are an individual, and your garden will be best if it reflects that individuality. This is far more important than your trying to make your garden designs acceptable, or "right," or your choosing plants that are "in." If you feel happy with a straight swath of lawn with deep, straight borders and a formal feature at its end, go for it! If winding paths and obscure secret places please you, look for ways to satisfy that need, keeping your mind and eye open for ideas.

Make sure you are happy with the shape, content, and size of your planned garden before beginning to dig, if possible, but be ready to change things as you grow in confidence. Sometimes it takes a while to discard old ideas and rethink an entire area, but when you have achieved a good balance among beds, house, trees, and plants, you will know it. You will be thrilled with your creation and be unable to look at it enough. You'll walk out with morning coffee, afternoon tea, and evening lemonade—even a flashlight at night—to enjoy it. Trust me, this happens. Put in a bench.

How to Begin

The first step, of course, is to choose the spot that most wants doing. Where do you really need a garden? Is your front entrance all it should be, or could it use a total revision—maybe even a new walk—in a different conformation? Do you have areas where the plants are in the wrong situation . . . say, shade plants in full sun, or an old sunny garden gone to shade? Have you lost a tree, so there's a perceived hole in your landscape, or a stump to disguise? Is there something you want to screen off? Some area where grass doesn't prosper?

Choose your site first, and then try very hard to envision the size, shape, proportions, and placement of the plants you wish to use, so you'll be able to make a bed that is the right size and shape. Doing this at the start of a new garden produces a result that gives you so much pride and satisfaction you will never neglect that step again.

PHOTOGRAPHY BY TOM COTTINGTON

The second year after we moved to this house, I planted a small slip of mountain ash by the mailbox. The locust tree was still a pretty, nonintrusive sapling, and the lawn was a typical subdivision-style sheet of grass. The gravel mulch, which I thought would set off the tree and the large rocks left by the builder, was not a good idea at all. Even with plastic underneath, the gravel caught detritus and dust, and soon fostered patches of weeds and grass, and it destroyed fingernails as I worked.

Outlining New Beds

My system for laying out beds is one that is disputed by many garden designers, but it satisfies some creative urge within me, and I believe it will work for many others. (Beth Chatto does it exactly this way!) If, like me, you wish to have sweeping curves and ovals, just get out there some evening with a long, flexible hose and outline the area you'd like to

The loss of the locust tree about ten years after we moved in inspired this low berm, which covers its knobby roots and ground-level stump. I imported soil and amended it with peat and manure. I brought in large, irregular rocks and set them in solidly to support the plants. The berm itself was pleasant, yet this new feature only called my attention more directly to the flaws already present in the landscape: the narrow, straight walk, the uninspired planting along the garage (those pink blossoms belong to the prolific annual *Impatiens balfourii*) and the patchy grass. I needed to change some big things.

Not until the sidewalk entrance along the porch had sunk about four inches a year later did I feel justified in having the walk torn up and replaced by a curving brick path. It was then that the front garden was really born.

change into a garden. If straight edges are your preference, you can mark off your proposed garden with lines of hose or anything straight and movable you can find: planks, hoe handles, lathes, two-by-fours, or bricks.

Then force yourself to do the following: go to bed and forget it. Get up in the morning and look out the window at the space. Do you still like it? Will it set off the plants you will put there? Does it still seem in proportion? Are there nice strong lines and clean curves, or is there a lot of weak vacillation in the outline? Go outside, back off to the edge of your property, and look at the space from several angles. What now? Does it show up from a distance? You want it to. Does it seem too dinky after all? Imagine tall plants

growing in it, and remember, tall plants spread out, as a rule, and take up a lot of room. Did you plan enough space to set plants of various smaller sizes around the tall ones—even when the plants are all mature?

Edging

One further consideration is important at the beginning. What kind of edge do you want your garden to have? When making straight-edged beds, you can choose to have permanent edging materials installed, such as ties, logs, rock wall, or some type of edging strip that can be sunk into the ground. If you choose any of the taller edgings, be aware that you will be faced with the eternal job of clipping back lawn grass from the outer edges. You will have to hand-trim around the sunken edgings, too, if you set them higher than the lawn mower blade; if you set them lower, grass will grow right over their tops to invade the beds, having to be pulled out. I do not like permanent edging (surprise!), but I suspect that is mainly because it defeats one of my most therapeutic garden activities: re-edging and reshaping beds and keeping them fluid and exciting. I do my re-edging with a sharp little border spade, slicing clean slanted troughs all around. Edges are cut frequently around here, often more than once a season, to control grass incursions or to enlarge and reshape. I don't mind. It is a way of freshening the picture and leads to other satisfying changes—a weed gone here, a plant moved there—which keep me in closer touch with the garden. The thin slices of sod I keep removing make good compost.

Using Rocks Well

Your garden will look more established if you incorporate some large, interesting rocks. The best time to do this, of course, is before you plant. I suppose this is one of my opinionated statements coming up, but bear with me. I am not talking about a rock garden, per se, or a tumble of boulders. Those are for experts. Here it is: unless you are building a garden around another bold existing feature, say a tree, a shrub, or an outcropping, you need to add some accent. The right rock, or rocks, can frame and set off your new garden beautifully, and it won't be as nice without such an accent. An elevated garden most of all needs a few "outcroppings," although a flat garden is equally enhanced by several large, low pieces, carefully placed, so that plants will arrange themselves around and over them gracefully.

The more closely you imitate nature in placing your rocks, the better the garden will look. If you make the effort to observe rock formations in nature or in the best rock gar-

Top: Hurray! I can't explain the feeling I had when the narrow, broken walk was gone at last, the new, curving bed for the bricks was leveled and tamped, and I had my hands on the heavy clay of the new bed. I dug and amended deeply and well, and the only mistake I made was in not raising the bed a foot or so for better drainage.

Bottom: For the first summer after putting in the walk, with all the excitement of planting the inner walk bed, I did not realize for a while that the whole picture was not making sense. Finally I realized: the berm was still an isolated crescent in green lawn. The garden beds were unsatisfying, separate elements, creating an interrupted, uncomfortable, stop-and-start path for the eye. I needed to unify those elements in order to create a welcoming entrance.

Left: **A natural-looking scree garden needs rocks. As in a natural setting, rocks collected together in one place should be of the same type and color and placed so that the strata, or grain, is the same in each piece, either on a horizontal or slightly canted plane. Selecting pieces of varying sizes is important for a natural look.**

Opposite: **The brick walk itself is much more satisfying, and the entrance more welcoming, now that the berm garden bed has been brought down to the brick edge, swept around the back of the curve, and settled into the landscape with rocks. The low, classical bench at the curve is precisely what I needed: a stopping place to rest and admire the ever-changing entrance garden. It is here that new plans are born, new gardens take shape, and old gardens are remade.**

dens, here is what you will see: all the rocks are of one color; the strata of all the rocks in any one area are parallel, either level with the horizon or all slightly tilted at the same angle; and the rocks themselves are settled well into the ground, usually with their flattest, broadest surface on top. They will not align themselves in straight rows or ring themselves around beds. They will not be evenly spaced, and they will never be found standing up on end, with a point sticking into the air! That is why flat sheets of limestone look well as stepping stones, outcroppings, or shelves, but not, for instance, as liners standing on edge around a fish pond. Gravity itself shakes down rocks into their most stable placement, and that is the way they look best. Note that naturally occurring rocks are partially buried in the soil, even to the leading edge.

To my eye, a border of boulders standing around a garden, however they are spaced and whatever their size, is not appealing—especially not rocks all of a similar size and shape. They have too much resemblance to oversized dentures. Even worse to look at are alternating rocks and plants: rock, plant, rock, plant, marching around a border or down a path. A better aesthetic balance is found in groups of rocks and plants both, with a bit of irregularity in size and shape to break the monotony.

Here I will really tread on some toes: a retaining wall of piled-up round boulders, all nearly the same size, can look like a giant bag of jellybeans. If your lot is part of a geological moraine and you already possess these glacial boulders, and if you really need a retaining wall, by all means use

Top: A north-to-south view of the path cut through the large bed under the young oaks shows the effect of curves with bold plantings. Even a short path laid out in this way lends mystery to a woodsy landscape. Any small new hosta babies are set here, on the humusy edges of the bark path in filtered light, to get acclimated to conditions for their first year. Only after they are strong enough are they taken out and placed in their new semipermanent homes. Hostas get moved many times as they grow.

Bottom: Cedar paths curve uphill toward the screened porch from the north, between dense greenery and colorful leafy borders in the old bark beds. White-variegated plants, trees, shrubs, hostas, and groundcovers are more important than flowers in these settings, bringing light and definition to the beds.

Opposite: Thick, soft paths of new cedar wood chips meander through the green growth of the north gardens in early summer, leading the eye to a distant prospect. Even the commonest of hostas is fresh and enticing along such a shaded path, set off with lamiums, sweet woodruff, ferns, hostas, and daylilies, with a common elderberry flowering in the background.

them. Just remember that in nature, gravity would have tumbled the largest to the bottom, and the wall would be uneven and broken by ledges, features, pockets, and plants, with smaller rocks filling up spaces between larger ones. Unfortunately, this is not a do-it-yourself kind of project, and you will have to depend on workers for the placement of these heavy features. Although you might not be popular with the front-end loader team you hire, you can try to have some effect on the way your wall is put together. Failing that, you can, I hope, at least find places to introduce a few plants to break up and soften the façade.

Making Paths

Paths are your best chance to show your individuality. These you will want to plan yourself, following your own natural trails through your property and using the material most sympathetic to you and your garden. Paths are both aesthetically and physically necessary in my gardens. I require accessibility at all times, for deadheading, dividing, replanting, or simply touching and sniffing every plant I grow. For these purposes, and for mystery and beauty, my paths wander and curve gently, often around tall, screening plants.

The paths that suit my woodsy back garden are soft and gray-brown, easy on bare feet and safe for shoes and boots. They are also fertile, and can be changed into planting beds in a flash. They are of bark. I like to use wood chips or bark because I can change the outline or move the whole path if I wish, with almost no work. Also, my paths are all on slopes, where soft paths work best.

But remember this advice about wood chips: if you want to use bark or chips for your pathways, it's better not to use summer tree trimmings with their green leaf content (way too fertile!), but to use plain chipped wood or bark gotten in winter or early spring. The more green stuff, the

A grass path sets off wide, open borders better than any man-made substitute. In this climate we have lawn grasses that stay soft and green all summer, unless there is a serious drought. I water only rarely, and then long and deeply. I do not use pesticides, so I get an occasional rash of ajuga, violet, or weed seedlings, which I pull. None of these would be objectionable in ones and twos, but, like rabbits, there is no such thing as one or two weeds in a lawn.

I have cut this wide path to curve and recurve like a green river between the two borders.

better the compost mix that evolves, and the more seedlings you will be hosting in your paths.

Recycling Bark Paths

Even with the cleanest wood chips, you will find in a couple of years that you have nicely decomposed humus in your paths and they've become fertile seedbeds. Seedlings of my precious primulas, aruncuses, and even hostas are often found nestled in the decomposed old bark of my paths after a few years. When this happens, I lift the seedlings and tuck them safely into beds, then I scrape the top four inches of soft humus off the paths, use it to mulch my beds or to make new beds, and put down new bark on the paths. Nothing is wasted. The adjoining gardens benefit as well as the paths, and the clean appearance is very pleasing.

It's especially pleasant to use cedar bark for paths; the aroma and reddish color are wonderful in the garden for the first month, and the gradual graying is attractive. Birch chips smell like root beer and make lovely paths also.

Plank walkways suggest marshes and water, and are beautiful crossing over streams or small ponds and straying through tall rushes. The graying wood is inviting and warm. Wooden rounds sliced from large logs are perfect in some situations, especially where paths curve and recurve, and they last a long time if properly treated with preservatives.

Stone or brick paths are beautiful when well planned, and I'd be happy with them in some places in my garden. But they are expensive and fairly permanent. Certain informal kinds of stone walks would work for me in the shady back garden, but not brick, which better suits a slightly more formal setting, such as my front entrance.

Grass paths are my favorites, and if you have the room, have them curve between rough-grown woodsy areas or between sunny borders. Wide, straight grass walkways are right for the rectangular garden; they lead the eye into the distance, offering an opportunity for a garden feature at the end of the vista. Whether your garden design calls for curved or straight lines, narrowing the lawn in places to form soft paths of green grass rests both eyes and feet as you traverse your garden. An inset island or berm bed should be near enough to one corner of the lawn so an even grass path is left to sweep around it; this works similarly to putting a painting in a good frame. All paths look best if they are wide enough for two to walk abreast, and if bordered with low plantings that fall irregularly over the edges here and there, with a few taller "see-through" plants to create mysterious nooks and crannies. A border with little plants stiffly staked at measured intervals is nervous and compulsive, and distracts the eye from the big picture. A natural, relaxed approach is both more beautiful and easier for the gardener.

Should You Call in a Landscaper?

If all these ideas make the thought of planning too daunting to begin alone and you feel you must have a landscaper's help with the initial layout, you should nevertheless be able to create your own unique and individual gardens. Search out a sympathetic landscaper. Talk to him or her about your needs, and be there during the walk-around and measurements. The best of them will work with you and be responsive to your taste. They will provide a comprehensive plan, dividing and shaping your spaces, and they can set up the planting program in annual increments if you desire. Landscapers know how to make your soil fertile and will suggest trees and plants. You can learn much from this process; just remember that you do not want your garden to reflect anyone's individuality but yours. More particularly, you do not want to overplant, putting in a garden that will obliterate itself in a few years. Listen to your landscaper's advice, but if you have done your homework, you will already know what you like, how it will look when mature, how much you are willing to care for and pay for, and at least a little about what will survive in your special garden.

If you have a brand new homesite to landscape, try to speak to the landscaper at a very early stage to allow for bringing in at least a foot of good, living soil to the areas where there will be garden beds. The usual inch of topsoil might be (barely) enough for sod or grass seed for the lawn, but it is cruelly insufficient for garden plants.

If you wish, a good landscape company can first remove unwanted trees, weeds, and grasses, grade and till difficult areas, and take care of the details of soil amendments, paths, terraces, steps, and mulches. Ideally, I suppose, it would be great to have all the rough preparatory work done professionally so you could just go ahead and plant your gardens, but this means that the entire landscape would need your immediate attention. To think of having all the gardens to plant at one time! Oh my. If you go for this approach, I suggest you simply have the trees put in at this time and perhaps a few key shrubs in several areas, but have most of the space put to rest under thick mulch while you work on your priority garden.

Unless you have a difficult situation, such as rough grading to be done or too many weed trees to remove, most everything is more satisfying if you do it yourself. You can do nearly everything, even the overall design, and the satisfaction of having done this is indescribable. It lasts a lifetime.

Care of the Soil

The art of gardening is to know your soil intimately, to treat it well and to select plants

which will make any soil seem like an asset, not a problem. You may not be able to grow

all the plants you would like to possess, but by choosing plants suited to your conditions

you can carpet the bare earth with contented plants rather than endure the effect

of a moth-eaten rug where too many plants have given up the struggle.

Beth Chatto, *The Green Tapestry*, Simon and Schuster, 1989

Removing Weeds and Grasses

MUCH HAS been written about creating good garden soil from poor. Poor soil is simply that which does not deliver nutrients in correct fashion to the plant roots. There can be any number of factors creating a poor delivery system, but it is still the basic element of poor soil. We might be tempted to say, for instance, that the soil is poor in a marshy spot, when in reality it is the gardener who is poor for attempting to grow plants there that require better drainage. Bog plants should grow luxuriantly in such a spot, with no amendments whatsoever. The same is true of thin soil in hot sun, or dry shade, or any other set of conditions that could drive us to despair. For best results, if you want a low-maintenance garden that will be naturally beautiful, look for those plants that need the conditions you can provide. Plants come from different environments, and they need very different conditions to thrive.

All soils need regular improvement. Mostly it is up to us to provide it in our gardens. If your soil is already growing lush weeds, it will probably make a pretty good garden for a year or so, needing little but removal of the weeds. Most soils need more than that as preparation for growing garden plants. Any soil will benefit from the addition of at least four inches of decomposed organic matter, forked as deeply into the surface soil as possible. A deep forking helps break up the compacted structure and allows air and moisture to penetrate. The newest information is that rototilling is too rough a treatment, turning up more weed seeds and disturbing things too much. I say, use your discretion: if you have a very large area to till, use the rototiller. A gentle turnover with a fork, burying the top layer along with the amendments, is best for smaller areas.

It is necessary to remove all growing material before making new beds and to prepare the edges so that such material will be discouraged from encroaching again. I have used several methods to take care of this necessary process. In the beginning, because I was always in a hurry for results, I laboriously dug out grass, then dug in amendments by hand. When I had lawn grass to deal with and felt I could wait over winter to start the new bed, I mowed it short, then spaded up deep blocks and turned them upside down, leaving the grasses and roots to decompose for a few months at the bottom of the spit. If, in either case, I was dealing with quack grass, creeping Charlie, or any other runner-rooted weed, I dug over the bed very deeply and thoroughly, removing every single inch of root before adding any amendments. Such beds should be left over winter, and a hard watch kept for weed sprouts from overlooked roots in the spring.

Many gardeners now feel that the organic method of plant removal is best: overlayering weeds or grass with either dark sheeting or very dense mulch, leaving the cover intact until the job is done. This method properly done kills quack or any other persistent weed or grass. Black plastic does this admirably, or sections of old carpeting, but for a thorough job lightproof coverings must be left in place for a year. Then they must be removed and the soil beneath them built up with amendments before planting. Multiple layers of newspaper make a cheap and biodegradable solution, if you give them at least a year, and they do not need to be removed. Lay them out five or six sheets thick (just the white printed pages, not the glossy or colored ones), wet them down with the hose, and apply a thick mulch of shredded bark. Begin to plant only when the bark has composted into soft soil; dig through the under layer of softened paper and add some of the composted bark to the planting holes.

Chemicals as a Last Resort

For a quicker solution, a good choice may be a product which kills all vegetation but leaches out of the soil quickly, killing grass in about two weeks. At that time, where the soil is basically good, turning the dead grass under with a spade may be all you need to do. The turned-under growth is wonderful "green manure," as long as every root is either dead, raked out, or buried very deeply; that is to say, a foot or more deep. (With quack grass, though, be certain to get every single inch of the root out, even if you think it is dead—it regenerates very rapidly!) If more amendments are needed, they may be layered and forked in after the grass is spaded under.

Even though such chemicals are touted as "biodegradable," I avoid their use because of the possible side effects on other forms of life. New information is surfacing all the time. After all, it took scientists many years to discover the deadliness of DDT.

A quick note: as soon as practical after such a dig-over, lay on a thick bark mulch or re-cover the site with sheeting to prevent weed seeds sprouting while you plan your plantings. If your plants are ready to add immediately, get the mulch around them quickly for the same reason.

Soil Tests

How do you know what amendments to add? There is a tendency to use far more fertilizer and pesticides than needed; lawn care businesses generally apply the maximum amount to every situation. Most of us know no better. Not only is the overuse of chemical materials bad for the ecology of the area, but also it can actually be harmful to your own plants. Every good teacher will tell you to have soil tests taken to discover what amendments are really needed. If you choose to have your local university school of agriculture do the testing, take samples from scattered locations in your growing area, digging down with the tubular sampler, or a trowel or shovel, eight to eighteen inches into the soil. Mix the samples all together. Then bag and label the resultant mix and take the bag to the testing station.

If you have a sour, undrained spot or a location where something odd is going on with the plant life, you should take a separate, small sample there. The inexpensive do-it-yourself soil test kits are fine. The results of either method will help you figure out the amounts and percentages of which nutrients to add. The process ensures that you add as little as possible, and only what is really needed. This point is terribly important; surplus nutrients do great damage when washed into the local ecosystem.

Organic Additives

No matter how terrible the soil, organic material alone makes a world of difference. It is the structure more than the content of garden soil that does the job. An open, light-textured soil with soft organic inclusions will support the greatest variety of plant life in good health. As organic materials break down, soil microbes and worms get to work, penetrating deeply into the soil beneath the layer without your having to dig it in. Enough organics can lighten and loosen stiff soil, improve water retention in sandy, loose soil, add bacteria and their resultant nutritional elements, and encourage worms to tunnel through, thus enriching and improving the soil in numerous ways. The lack of organic material will cause great distress to plants, or even their failure, despite the presence of all the mineral nutrients. Newer inorganic soil additives are available that open and aerate soil very nicely, and they should be used at times, but not to the exclusion of good rotted organic matter. I recommend soil testing, but even if you do not get around to taking samples, you can grow a perfectly respectable garden if you add organic matter

Page 24: Very little of the fall leaf mulch has been removed from this bed, which lies at the eastern edge of a woods, looking westward onto the lawn. When daffodil leaves first poke up underneath such dense cover, it becomes immediately obvious where there will be trouble: steep tents of matted leaves form quickly over the growing stems. These tents must be broken up, or daffodils will bleach and buckle as they try to reach the sun.

The bulk of the leaves are left to decompose into the garden, where they encourage earthworms and healthful microorganisms and also serve to keep the soil moist. By fall these leaves will all have been converted to humus and have disappeared into the soil.

and then fertilize much more lightly than package instructions. Trouble spots should definitely be tested.

These methods are always worth the work—and I write as one with arthritic knees, a touchy back, and incipient carpal tunnel problems. I have at least one (very) large pile of bark and one of manure delivered every year, and I haul it by cartloads and spread it myself. You can do it if I can, and you might even enjoy it.

Be Creative

What may surprise you is how creative you can be in introducing organic material into a garden area if you do it well before putting in any plants, and if you give it time to "mellow." An article published in the 1850s told of one gardener who buried old leather shoes and old cotton and wool clothing in his raspberry patch as a means of getting organic material into the soil! This wouldn't work with today's synthetics, but it gives you the idea.

I use a wide variety of materials at different times to enrich the soil: manures, compost, chopped bark, rice hulls, leaves, chopped branches, and even raw garbage at times. I bury "green manure" in small garden patches every year, either sod dug under at least twelve inches, or lawn clippings (watch out not to use clippings from a lawn treated with broadleaf killer!) or chopped leaves and garden waste. I sometimes dig out a tired garden patch or a newly planned garden site about two feet deep and use it as a compost pit for soft materials for a couple of months, then close it up in the fall. The following spring is time enough to add plants. This method is especially effective when dealing with the area close to the foundation walls of a house, where builder's detritus has probably ruined the soil for growing anyhow. In that case, throw away the dug-out dirt (it's okay to call such trash "dirt" instead of "soil"!). I also dig holes around certain plants all during the warm weather and bury kitchen waste (and small dead animals) in them. Peonies thrive on this treatment, and shrub roses too, especially with banana peels in the garbage.

Repeat Warning

This is a good place to say once more that the compacted and microbially dead area around a brand new house isn't going to grow anything with sizable roots for at least a year in any case. This is why so much of a builder's "foundation planting" around new houses has to be replaced so quickly. Much better to use deep, deep layers of bark and a lot of benign neglect for a year or so until the worms and microbes have had a chance to move in. Annuals, because of their shallow roots, will grow and give you a summer's worth of color and greenery there if you really need it.

Composting

The most important organic practice you can learn to do from the beginning is to make good compost, which will turn unproductive dirt into good soil in short order. Compost can be produced in mounds, trenches, barrels, or bins as long as it has enough sun to warm the pile, and I find it does not require turning. It is very difficult for me to lift and turn heavy compost heaps, so I had to discover a method that eliminates this process. The key is kitchen waste. If you keep a small, covered pail of some kind in the kitchen and put into it all your vegetable waste in a little water, you will find that it heats up quite rapidly. This hot material is the catalyst for "starting" a compost heap. Layer manure and green vegetative material, sod, and chopped leaves in the compost pit or bin, dig holes in the layers each time you carry out a pailful of waste (this is why you keep the pail small, as you will soon discover), and cover the pockets of hot waste with the layered stuff. When you have a large mound, bury the waste in different spots all over the surface. You won't need "compost starter" or fertilizer or any other fancy treatment, and you will wind up with crumbly, delicious-smelling humus. It is one of the nicest miracles of nature.

Chop Before Composting

Complete green plants, roots and all, may be thrown on the compost heap whole, though not those with woody stems, especially if you plan to turn the compost regularly. Chopping large-scale lawn and garden waste before layering it in, however, really speeds the process. I have even used finely chopped tree branches and leaves. The big mechanical chippers produce fine quality compost fodder, though they are expensive and, I think, dangerous to use. Professional tree trimmers use good chippers. They, as well as your city's tree-trimming service, have to take their chopped branches to a dump site to get rid of them; a telephone call can often have the trucks dump this material in your driveway instead, at no charge. Any insects or diseases that may have come with this crop will be destroyed when it heats up and composts. If it is July and very hot, you'll be surprised how quickly this stuff begins to "work"! Whenever I have such chipped material dumped on my hot asphalt driveway I let it rest for a month or so, and it becomes quite hot in that time. The green leaves add considerably to the nutritional value of the wood chips, and this decomposed material is wonderful as is around plants. If you use the tree waste right away, remember that the finishing stages of composting draw lots of nitrogen from the soil. So add a good high-nitrogen fertilizer to the garden underneath such wood chips to prevent chlorosis (a common 10-10-10 lawn mixture works). Be sure, too, that the ground is well watered before you lay down any compost; otherwise the compost

layer will be prolonging a dry condition.

Chips are lightweight, and a very large cartful is easy enough to push, uphill or down, to where it can be dumped on beds, paths, or the compost heap. When I have very finely shredded bark, I keep a small pile handy to add to the compost heap during the summer, in increments, alternating with garden cuttings and manure.

Manure Is Gardener's Gold

When building up the organic content of soils, besides garden waste and compost, the finest material to use is manure, as old and rotten as possible, and any kind you can find. I use one kind one year, another the next. A horse or pony farm in your area may be able to bring you a load or two, and many farming areas have cow manure heaps, which are available without charge. While I prefer to have things truck-delivered, I know many gardeners who fetch their manure in trash bags, making as many trips as it takes. Rabbit and poultry manure is wonderful, so look for kids in the neighborhood who have rabbit hutches. Many years I have simply bought bags of composted sheep, poultry, or cow manure and layered it on two inches thick around my perennials, especially around the shrub roses. It does not smell, and it quickly gives a sweet, mellow odor and texture to the soil. Here, too, it may be wise to rotate the kinds of packaged manures you use. I have had no visible ill effects from any bagged manures I purchased, but diversity should take care of any slight contamination of one kind or another. It would be wonderful if we could be assured that some available manure products were "purely organic"; that is, from animals not given chemicals.

Horse droppings sometimes do present problems with pasture weed seeds. It is good to check on how old the supply is before you have it delivered. Get last year's pile if you can.

Peat Moss and Its Alternatives

Peat moss is the material most traditionally used around here to amend poor soils, but peat bogs are being rapidly depleted. I like to use other materials when I can, though some things, like beds of rhododendrons or astilbes, really need the acidity and texture of peat. For a brand-new garden, it is necessary to load on all amendments thickly, at least two and preferably three or four inches thick, then fork in the mixture. Because I have such heavy clay, this takes a lot of peat moss. As a substitute, I like to use manure, cottonseed meal, or rice hulls to till into new beds, and often use coarse sand as well—though not just any kind of sand, as fine stuff makes clay into cement. You need to use coarse builder's sand or "sharp" sand. I discovered that even if I merely spread a layer of this sand over the surface of a clayey bed, it makes a difference in a year or so; it seems to work its way down, probably because I dig up, divide, and replant things so often.

Should You Import Mixed Soil?

There are times it isn't worthwhile to attempt to amend your own soil. If your situation is as impossible as what I found in many parts of my scraped-down yard, and if you have terrible drainage, the best solution may be to have some soil mixed to your specifications and hauled in by the yard for a raised garden. Several nurseries in my area will put equal parts topsoil, sand, and manure in their blending tumbler and deliver it. They also blend equal parts builder's sand, rice hulls, and pea gravel for a fast-draining rock garden soil, which resembles the scree that many alpine plants require. I have used both of these mixes in different situations, and believe me, it beats blending by hand, and you will soon forget the cost. I have found that two yards makes quite a thick mound for a raised bed, about six feet wide and nine feet long, where I can vary the height and incorporate some big feature stones to set off the plantings. Three yards makes a nice deep, large garden berm. Just remember, new soil sinks, so make the berm somewhat higher than your plan.

The benefits of this more expensive treatment are manifold: for instance, before having any soil delivered you do not have to spade up the entire area where your garden will be located. You can leave the grass in place in the center—where the new soil will bury it at least a foot deep—as green manure. You can further build up the center and at the same time discourage the surrounding lawn from making incursions by cutting a sharp edge about a foot wide, all around the planned berm, digging up the sod and throwing the clumps upside-down into the middle of the garden, to be covered by the imported soil. Covering the sod you've cut with about a foot of the mixed soil gives your new plants room to have a well-drained upper root structure, while giving nutritious support to deeper roots.

With a gritty sand mixture, the pea gravel works its way to the surface and creates those all-important gravel collars that prevent crown rot.

Top Dressing

A top dressing is a layer of organic material that serves as a mulch to hold moisture. A top dressing of two inches of peat moss, rice hulls, cocoa bean hulls, manure, shredded leaves, or finely shredded bark should be added to established gardens at least every other year in late spring. It should be laid down just before the heaviest growth appears, while there is still room around the bases of plants, say in early June, before the ground hardens with summer heat but after spring rains have deeply moistened the soil.

If the rains have been scarce, make sure to water thoroughly before mulching; no mulch should be laid over dry soil. This treatment keeps the soil from "capping," or forming the hard crust that sheds water so effectively, and it allows a moisture-retentive layer to form. This layer promotes worm and bacterial activity, making for a deep, loamy soil. You will be surprised how rapidly good soil can be built by regular mulching. Just remember that laying mulch over dried-up soil does harm, not good, because it tends to keep the soil from improving.

The most immediate effect of summer mulches is the reduction of seeded weeds. I do not hoe weeds, by the way. I pull them. If I had lots of space between plants, I might weed shallowly with a scuffle hoe, but maybe not. Every single inch one turns up in the garden holds weed seeds or gives shelter to new ones. I try not to disturb the soil as I hand-pull every weed. Weeds will seed, to a certain extent, in any mulch, but they have declined dramatically over the years because I get them out before they set seeds.

A light top dressing should be applied in the fall to new or reworked beds, especially if you plant bulbs. Do this after the ground is frozen, if possible; it helps keep the soil from thawing and refreezing. This mulch may be scratched into the beds the next spring to condition the soil. The top dressing I prefer for this application is very finely shredded bark, placed about two inches deep on beds that have been raked clear of leaves. A light dressing of peat moss or manure may be used in this way as well. Such applications do not take the place of a marsh hay winter covering for new or sensitive plants; hay may be lightly layered over any of them. Hay is not a top dressing in my garden, just a protectant. It must be removed in spring. The trick is to remove only the hay, not the mulches.

For woodland beds, most years I simply pile on several inches of lawnmower-chopped grass and leaves. I remove only enough of them in the spring to allow the ephemerals

and daffodils enough light and air to come up. The rest of the leaves are allowed to decompose naturally. This treatment has gradually given me excellent, humusy soil in the woodland areas.

The Perils of Plastic

Here is another of my warnings, from experience: I definitely do not recommend using plastic sheeting under organic mulches. The benefit of a good mulch is to enrich the soil beneath it, as I have said, and plastic prevents that. Far more important, you do not discourage weeds with a plastic sheet; quite the opposite. Water trapped on the plastic will soften and compost the organic mulch very quickly, forming a perfect seed bed for anything that comes along, so that in one season you will have a big crop of weeds, in two, a jungle, and in three you will have to rip out the plastic plus a ton of soil and a solid mass of weed roots.

Gravel Mulches

Gravel mulches are becoming popular around here, I think because homeowners are seeing them in commercial settings where intensive maintenance keeps the gravel clean and clear. That's a mighty tempting sight—but it's an illusion. Most landscapers place gravel over plastic sheets. See above. Weeds grow in gravel! There are fiber sheets to lay under gravel mulch that allow water to drain and don't let seedlings grow through from beneath, and you certainly can use them. Just be warned: you will still have pockets of dust, dirt, and decomposed vegetation that will settle in the gravel quite rapidly and sponsor forests of seedlings. These must be hand-pulled or sprayed with chemicals several times per season.

Use gravel mulches if you really like them, but this is not the best way to surround shrubs or perennials anyhow, unless you can leave an open ring around the plants for the addition of needed organic materials and if you are willing to do the work of weeding.

"Gravel gardens" are showing up everywhere, and I hate to see them proliferate. Even when people manage to take perfect care of the weed problem, they often make poor choices in gravel types. White or very light gravel beds are glaring and ugly to me, and they are so light-reflective that despite the coolness they bring to roots, they cause leaf-burn in full sun. I have even seen hostas stuck in such gravel patches, and I can't look at them without cringing. Red, gray, or brown gravel is easier on the eyes and on the plants, but even so it makes a garden look to me as if it belongs in front of an insurance building. Gravel can be used artistically but usually isn't. Around shrubs, trees, and evergreens, as long as one remembers to renew the circle of organic mulch around each annually by scraping back and then replacing the gravel collar, a gravel bed is okay. Just remember that this is definitely not a method for eliminating weeds, if that is your objective.

What to use instead? Crushed stone or shells are good, but bark is lighter, cheaper, more recyclable, easier on weed-pulling fingers, and much more attractive and natural, especially in a woodsy setting.

Fertilizers and Pesticides

I need to make my position really clear on fertilizers and pesticides. You would expect me to say of fertilizers that organic is not only better, but it is the only way. I am more middle-of-the-road on that subject: organic always seems best to me because it will not burn, but it makes perfect sense that a fertilizer is only as good as its chemical components, and those are available in commercial blends. They work as well as organic ones, though I think they should be applied much more sparingly than the package directs, and attention should definitely be paid to the requirements of your soil.

This is probably a good time for another tip born of painful experience: do not take verbatim any statement about a plant's needs that is not based on the specifics of your region and its soil. For example, I added lime, based on many general writings about clematis, and watched my healthy vines go from chlorotic to dead in two years. The clay soil in my part of southern Wisconsin is already alkaline, and more calcium simply blocks the absorption of iron. Those vines shaded one end of a big screened porch. I miss them. The only remedy has been to dig out a deep block the size of a grave (very symbolic) and replace the damaged soil with compost and fresh topsoil. New vines are in place, but I still mourn the thick vines that a soil test would have saved.

For fertilizing perennials, I use a standard 5-10-10 mixture about half- or quarter-strength, over the whole garden when planting a new bed, and I leave most of my plants on their own after that, unless something visibly declines. Certain things, like peonies and clematis, I fertilize lightly in spring, with a dry 5-10-10 scattered around the drip line.

About pesticides I have stronger feelings. I do not allow "prevention" treatments to be put on lawn or garden. Would you take medicine full-time just in case you might get a virus or two? Think what poisoning grubs does to the earthworms, and then to the birds! And what it does, eventually, to our ground water. Excess fertilizer is equally harmful, ending up in choked streams and lakes. Watchful moderation is what I say. Turf that is lightly fed, seldom but deeply watered, and mowed at the proper height is pretty good at choking out weeds, and it stays healthy, too. A garden full of vigorous, healthy plants has no room to spare for weeds, either. With certain trees I have been taking occasional chemical prevention measures simply because there are diseases in nearby trees that would spread, and that have destroyed trees for me in the past. I don't mess with the lawn and garden, however, until I see real need. My shrub roses get a dose of systemic rose fertilizer and insecticide in the spring, and a pailful of light Epsom-salt solution in June when I apply the fresh mulch.

Seasonal Cleanup

The fall and spring cleanup of the perennial garden is highly important to the health of the plants, but it is still open to interpretation. Certain parts of a cleanup cannot be left undone: peony, phlox, and German iris foliage, for instance, need to be cut back and removed in the fall (remembering not to cut down the tree peony stems!) because of overwintering diseases, insects, and molds. The debris should be carried out with the bagged trash rather than used for compost. As for the rest of the cleanup, some gardeners put it off entirely until spring, leaving the stems and fallen leaves to catch snow and to shade and protect the roots. Some clear out messy undergrowth but leave some tall stems for snow-catching and bird-feeding. Some clean the garden to a spic-and-span austerity. I have been known to leave my garden in any of these three conditions in any given winter, though not often the last. I can't really say that any of these leads to a better garden the following spring, though I have found that the cleaner I make the area, the more I need to apply an airy mulch in the fall, such as marsh hay, to protect things from emerging too early and getting bitten in a thaw-freeze situation in spring.

We all know the big drawback if we follow the "leave it for the birds" theory in fall: we have to make time for finishing the cleanup the next spring. It is a firm fact that the cleaner the garden at the beginning of the growing season, the easier it is to care for. In a clean garden, it is that much easier to remove grass roots and weeds, to lift and divide overgrown plants, to remove excess plants, and even to put

down the summer mulch.

It is always much busier around here in spring than fall, what with everything happening at once, and I'm always aware of that going into the winter season, so I do try to get spring cleanup down to a manageable level. So I cut back all the really tall things in fall: thalictrums, plume poppies, meadowsweets, the tall aruncus, kirengeshoma, artemisia, Culver's root, poppies, yarrows, tall lilies, Solomon's seal, daylilies, Siberian iris, and monarda. Anything tall and stiff goes in the big, loose compost pile in back of the shed. If I had a better chopper, I tell myself, I might get these all reduced to small bits and loaded in the compost barrel. Maybe I would. When the green has gone out of some of the lower-growing things, like the geraniums, heucheras, astilbes, and so on, I cut those, and they do wind up in the compost barrel.

Winter Protection

Winter protection is a fact of life up here in the north. Zone 4, with a low of -30 to -20 degrees, is the safest designation to look for when buying perennials, though much of the area is Zone 5, or -20 to -10 degrees. Remember, our winters often approach the Zone 3 level of -40 to -30 for short periods! Many woodies and perennials need absolutely no extra care at all, because they are native or from other places just as rugged. Yet even those plants may have been changed and perhaps softened by the amount of fertilizer that seeps in from surrounding plantings and by the surfeit of water they receive as part of the garden. In the wild, they would have tougher love, and would be sending their roots deeper in order to survive. As shallower-rooted, protected plants, they may need some winter protection, especially in their first winter or two.

In the garden, protection is especially important for

Hiding within this burlap shroud is *Hydrangea quercifolia* 'Silver Queen', a Zone 6 shrub that freezes back so much each winter that it almost never sets bloom for me. I have begun wrapping it after a good freeze with burlap, held on a metal framework constructed of folding plant supports.

I always pray the gardener's prayer over this burlap tent: that this winter the plant will come through with no freeze-back, because it has been strengthened by good growth for a whole year, and I am protecting it.

ground is well frozen and the weather is so cold that we have to pull scarves up over our red noses and wear thick mittens and stocking caps before we go out to cover the garden. That's just one of the minuses of Zone 4 gardening. But it's good for the plants. Gives you a warm, virtuous feeling, too, once it's over, so it's good for you, also.

In that rare winter when temperatures stay warm into December, we sometimes have to lay down mulches before a freeze—but we do it as late as we can, and then with misgivings, hoping for a quick freeze and a good snow cover.

My enemy is the big, deep, surprise snowfall before the ground is frozen and before I have laid mulch. What a mess then; what to do? I usually wait—either the snow melts and I can attack the mulch problem later, or the snow stays on and keeps coming down, becoming deep enough to last until the true spring thaw, which solves the problem. If all should melt in a January thaw, I am out of luck. I will never be able to dig up the icy thatches of leaves from the north corners of the frozen yard, and unless I have enough Christmas tree branches to protect the tenderest things, I am going to lose some plants.

There is a minimalist solution, one I follow in very busy years: give the garden as a whole only a very light mulch covering, early on, after cleanup, so that air can circulate and normal freezing can take place. Marsh hay is best, well aerated, but an inch of shredded bark or manure will do all right, or even a light shredded-leaf cover. The more tender Zone 5 and 6 plants, or any new garden areas, are perhaps enough to worry about after freezing, when you can go out and give them a nice overcoat of Christmas tree branches, or leaf mulch, or a burlap wrap.

Above all, beware of laying down thick, heavy clumps of mulch at any time, as air and light are necessary to all plants and bulbs starting their growth in spring; and a too-warm,

newly planted bulbs and perennials. The best plan is to use extremely lightweight materials, either marsh hay, straw, or evergreen boughs laid over the frozen beds in an airy layer, with light branches to hold them down. These materials must of course be watched closely in spring and removed gradually, as the new little plants need light to develop but will freeze if protection is removed too early.

When to Apply Winter Mulch

I wish to stress here, even though I'm sure it's common knowledge: winter protection is not used to prevent plants from freezing—it is applied to keep things frozen. Therefore, it is not good practice to pile on mulches and add rose cones while the ground is still warm. For one thing, voles love the protection and might have a chance to gnaw your rose stems clear through. We gardeners like to wait until the

dark environment will start whitish, weak shoots, which sap the plants and sometimes kill them. For this same reason, do not weigh down mulch with planks.

Protect Woodies Too

In their first year or so, it can't hurt to protect the upper growth of woodies and evergreens with burlap and to pile an airy mulch over their roots after the ground has frozen. Evergreens have a tendency to burn from winter wind and sunlight, and a windscreen-shade should be set up to protect them for several winters, at least. To prevent damage, anti-desiccants may be sprayed on evergreens when they are a bit older. It's always a gamble to omit these small jobs. In some milder winters, an unprotected tree may come through undamaged, but then a dry, windy spell might come in early spring that utterly destroys a precious tree. In other words, you might get by without extra protection, though I don't recommend it.

The one thing you must not skip is plentiful fall watering; evergreens and woodies should go into winter well watered. After watering, I mulch the area under all of my small trees out as far as the branch tips to prevent heaving. I often use manure; it does not deplete nitrogen as uncomposted bark does.

What Happens to All the Mulch?

And what does one do with all that mulch come spring? I usually have the woodsy gardens piled so deeply with chopped leaves that they are wet and compacted by April, and I must loosen and remove a good part of them to allow the spring growth to come up. But I never remove all the mulch. It is too nourishing to the soil. I stir and aerate the last inch or two, after I have gently removed, by hand, the compressing upper layers. I like the work. Much new growth is still

invisible underground but will come up through this light cover. If you do the same, and watch during the summer, you will see this thinner layer disappear completely as worms haul it underground and various bacteria set about digesting it. The mulch I remove goes on my compost heap.

Now You Are Ready to Plant

I have almost—almost, please note—given up buying plants on impulse,

as I've gotten so fed up with not being able to find a good place for them.

I hate the way they glower at me from their pots, reproaching me for my greed.

Anne Wareham, "Moral Extremes in the Garden," in *The Hardy Plant*, Autumn 1997
(journal of the Hardy Plant Society)

THE GREATEST TRICK in our northern gardens is to maintain a constant flow of leaf and blossom all season long, and to have the changing display remain attractive and mutually complementary. Each plant should be showcased when at its best, and either be attractive or unobtrusive in between. It is not difficult to accomplish this if you do your homework. You need to learn the conditions favored by the plants you choose so you will know better than to set a moisture-lover into dry sand, or a desert plant into forest loam, or an alpine into stiff clay. It is also important that you learn the bloom times of your favorites so you can make combinations in the garden that will enhance one another perfectly.

While some plants have a wide range of tolerance as to conditions, others are awfully fussy. Within each category of soil and light tolerance, look into the sizes and shapes of plants you would like to use or combinations that are pleasing to you. Visits to area gardens will sharpen your eye for such associations. Visit several times during the growing season, watching the succession of dominant plants, and see where they grow best and make the best show. Make friends with good gardeners, and talk to them when you are in their gardens. Ask them about favorite combinations, growing conditions, and special methods of propagation or care. And remember, in gardening as in real estate, it's location, location, location!

Cannibal Plants

One of the best things experience teaches is to avoid plants that overwhelm other growing things. Many such plants are offered in catalogs without footnotes, which seems reprehensible to me, though it is true that the rampant characteristics of some plants vary in different areas, so a plant that becomes a pest in our conditions might be a modest garden subject in the desert. In most cases you can at least avoid those plants with the word vigorous in the description; dealers are willing to go that far to give you a clue. Some of the following pesky plants are absolutely lovely in bloom and perfectly proportionate to the garden when very young, but all have exhibited takeover propensities in my garden.

I say, never plant *Lythrum salicaria*, gorgeous as it can be, both because it will seed into the gutters and sewers and infest native marshlands, and because it will take over your garden beds.

Physostegia virginiana, obedient plant, is lovely with its pink-purple spikes of little snapdragon flowers, and even more so in its white form, but it will crowd out even daylilies when in full growth.

Houttuynia cordata 'Chameleon' makes pretty tricolored ivylike leaves, and is so attractive when six inches tall that you might be tempted to use it as a border plant. But watch out! It will be eighteen inches tall and thick as grass when happy, and its roots are very deep and greedy. This is a plant to perhaps be used as groundcover for a difficult slope somewhere, but not as a companion plant.

Lysimachia clethroides, or gooseneck loosestrife, makes the nicest recurving spikes of white pearls in the garden, but its roots are even greedier than those of the houttuynia. Gooseneck grows about two feet tall, and it blossoms with a galaxy of white cones all curving in the same direction. The bloom stems are wonderful in bouquets, of course; so I keep a colony of gooseneck in a back corner, in a bit too much shade. It survives.

The fern-leaved tansy is a plant that not only spreads rapidly through the roots but also has overwhelming, thirty-inch, flopping top growth; hence, pretty as its thick, crimped ferny leaves are, it is not a good garden subject for me.

Campanula glomerata has balls of intense purple-blue

Page 36: Once the garden is established and the long-planned plant combinations have begun to move through their successive seasonal patterns, it becomes absolutely necessary to have a place to sit down once in a while—to just look. A bench in the right spot is essential.

Garden time is very precious. A perfect picture glimpsed and then put off until later—"when there's more time"—is nearly always gone or changed before we go to look at it again. Taking time for short breaks or just sitting quietly brings one closer to the garden, close enough to see the ladybugs and butterflies, to check on the toads, and watch the newest buds unfurl.

flowers, and it even reblooms after the first flush is over, but it chokes out other plants and takes over entire beds.

The species *Lamiastrum galeobdolon* gives the lamium family its bad name for rampant spreading. It will actually take over an entire forest floor, blanketing over the tops of any plants under a foot in height and winding up into taller things. It has pretty green and silver leaves and yellow pea-blossoms, but you do not want it in a garden bed.

I also caution you not to invite into your planned beds any of the wild goldenrods, buttercups, or Queen Anne's lace. You are warned.

War on Weeds?

Another of my pet notions is that native "weeds" should be respected. Often they occupy an important niche in the ecology. Just to take one as an example, I have learned to leave some stinging nettles *(Urtica)* growing in out-of-the-way places for butterfly larvae. Strangely, these inhospitable-seeming itchy plants are host to the larvae of several species of butterfly, most noticeably, in my garden, Milbert's Tortoiseshell, which has a pattern actually resembling its name, in dark brown-black with yellow and orange bands and spots. It is unmistakable and lovely, and I enjoy knowing when I see it that it is in my neighborhood because I bothered to leave a few nettles in my borders. The rusty-colored Comma butterfly also uses nettles as egg and chrysalis sites, and provides two broods in a good year. Most spectacular of all, and more rarely seen, the Red Admiral also prefers nettle to other food plants. This butterfly is an unforgettable sight, barred with hot orange-red on black.

The ecology of our suburban areas is so fascinating and so fragile that I think we have done great harm by our "clean house" attitude about what we call weeds. And in the case of the nettle, it is not an ugly plant to look at, once you clear

PHOTOGRAPHY BY TOM COTTINGTON

your mind of the "weed" epithet. Just cut off its seed heads to keep it in bounds—and do be careful when handling it. I am certain there are other wild plants with useful characteristics that we might find room for. I do not suggest that we leave our lawns waste places, but why not look into the habitat requirements of beneficial and beautiful creatures, and try to accommodate them into our lives? Life will be poorer when they are gone.

Monitor Changing Conditions

Conditions have a way of changing in small local patches, and even the best gardener can sometimes go on struggling too long with a bad situation. I recently realized that I have been trying for several years to conceal, cut off, or give enough water to a suffering planting of lady fern and hostas in the crowded, dry root area of the neighbor's huge locust tree and my Norway maple. When I looked at this dried-up area one summer, it finally hit me: how many years have I been telling people they should make their plantings suit the conditions? I have followed my own advice, and now enjoy a

This is the dread houttuynia, which has caused not one but several foot-deep reworkings of the bed near the brick walk to get it out, and it is still hiding roots all the way under a wide granite boulder. These very beautiful leaves do not stay in low, polite ground-cover form, but get a good eighteen inches tall, smothering out daylilies and reaching up into shrub branches. Their roots go deep in long-reaching and branching channels a foot underground, which does not allow companion plants to flourish. They are not friendly but are terrible bullies. Initially I thought that if I did not like them after a year, I could just pull them up. Wrong.

Top: There is no blue richer or more welcome in the garden than that of the purplish-blue balls of *Campanula glomerata*, though I am the first to say that one can have too much of a good thing. Not the blue—there could never be too much of that —but the growth habit of this plant is very piggy. This bed is in dire need of cleaning out and reworking.

Bottom: The long-overdue garden revision took place in the summer of 1998. I dug about nine-tenths of the crowded plants out of this bed, including a bushel or so of violets and branched coneflower, gave some away and divided and replanted others. *Lamiastrum galeobdolon* creepers were also cut back in the neighbor's bed to prevent further incursions. I then amended the soil with manure and peat.

I replanted good divisions of the daylilies, and a few *Heuchera* 'Pink Pewter' were added at the front for an eye-catching border. To take advantage of the dryness and the noon sunlight, I chose tall grasses for the back, *Miscanthus zebrinus*, or zebra grass, being the most outstanding. This I used in three clumps, to catch the light and the breeze and to frame the garden. Several clumps of *Hakonechloa macra* function in the mid-foreground to pick up the gold in the taller grass.

whole new and exciting garden, cleansed of the knotted roots of spreading plants, better laid out, and filled with more xeric plants and grasses that can take both sun and shade.

Moving Plants Around

Nothing will save you from making mistakes. You can't absorb it all at once. You are, after all, a gardener. Gardeners are well known for overoptimism! Anyhow, mistakes are only food for further change. Anything that can be planted can be moved. You need not be afraid to dig up and rearrange your groupings until they are pleasing to you.

And yes, it is possible to dig up some things in bloom, even in midseason, if you get a deep shovelful of dirt with the roots. But you must first dig the hole where the plant will be put, loosen the soil at the bottom, and fill the hole with water. Set the plant clumps very firmly, tromping them down and watering them in, and do not try to divide any of them if it is midsummer. In spring, do the dividing when green is just showing above ground; don't wait for tall stems. At this time you may separate into divisions, and remember to dig holes for any of them you wish to replant, following the same procedure as above. Fall divisions are made after cutting back the stems to about four or five inches before digging, and after getting the planting spots ready. In any season, it is good to divide and plant on a rainy day, or at least in the evening.

Many plants hate to be moved: hellebores, monkshoods, peonies, and so on. I am happy to say this, though; nearly all plants are more adaptable than you think. For those of you who put plants in the wrong spot and think you have to watch them struggle and die, I have cheery news: most plants can be moved around like furniture without harm! Even rose bushes! Watch the symptoms: if you know a plant should be having lots of bloom, but it isn't doing

much at all in spite of your having followed soil, watering, and fertilizing instructions, and if it looks weak and leans toward the light, move it! It wants more sun! If a plant has burnt edges, toughened and shrunken leaves, and a rubbery appearance, chances are it is in too much sun and would love a little more cool shade, especially in the afternoon.

You should be encouraged to play around with your materials and find the combinations that work for you. Most plants can be moved at any time, some even when they are in bloom. All you have to remember when moving midseason is: move plants whole, with a good rootball, into a prepared spot, and water in well. Moving on a rainy day, especially toward evening, is a wise plan too, and sometimes it is necessary to give some artificial shade for a day or two.

A Garden from a Dump?

Increasingly you will learn how to make the most of your available area and acquire a sharper eye for that neglected corner, that bedraggled bed, or that bare patch.

If there is a genuine waste place on your property, where cement blocks, cinders, or even trash have been dumped for years, you soon will be viewing it with a newly discriminating eye: maybe if you kill the weeds with a black tarp for a few months, then start with a load of mixed soil here and a couple of good boulders there, you can create a really smashing rock garden!

Nothing I do as a gardener gives me more satisfaction than to turn a really dull or ugly spot into a place of beauty. Take some of the attention you lavish on your spectacularly successful beds and look around you. I guarantee you will find areas that can be lifted out of the humdrum into interesting backgrounds, or even into stunning features, with a bit of thought. You will be surprised how little it takes sometimes: maybe just one small tree or vine to cover an eyesore, or a freshly cut border and a curve of attractive plants around a corner, or perhaps one bold feature plant. As your garden builds, the plants required for these makeovers will usually be right under your nose. In fact you will often discover you have made over two areas with one switch: thinning out one overgrown area and setting up a new plant grouping elsewhere. Inevitably this activity leads to further refinements, changes in adjacent areas, and—eventually—new beds and new purchases.

Actually, I think I just described the whole machinery of becoming a gardener!

Perennials Need Care

My final admonition is that a perennial bed is not a do-it-once-and-forget-it deal. Not only is there the constant activity described above, but also perennials multiply, and most need division every two or three years. They deplete their soil and need lots and lots of organic material to keep them in good health. And once every seven to ten years or so it is beneficial to dig the whole bed up—excluding those few deep-rooted things such as shrubs and peonies that object to such treatment—replenish the soil deeply, divide the good plants, tear out the pirates, and replant the entire garden along whatever lines you can envision. The results of such a reworking will be very pleasing to you, for many reasons. You will have had time to become more selective, for one thing, and you have perhaps managed to learn how to please some spectacular plants (say, delphiniums!). Or you will have discovered that a larger grouping of a certain color is needed, or that something you are growing in another area of your garden would look better here. Moreover, you will have hundreds of divisions to sell at your club's plant sale or to give to other gardeners. And a brand new garden to contemplate. Another new bench!

Page 41: This is the south or street edge of the crowded garden with the *Campanula glomerata* before revision. Tall prairie plants have multiplied, choking off light and nourishment from the entire bed. Coneflowers and globe thistles have seeded around and come up everywhere they pleased, and tall asters and meadowsweets have almost choked out the daylilies and other plants from behind. Definitely time something was done.

Trees, Shrubs, and Vines

People often ask me: "What is your favorite garden?" I reply, "Whichever one I'm working in."

Marlyn Dicken Sachtjen, *Marlyn's Garden*, Chicago Review Press, 1994

F I LEAVE YOU with only one imperative, I hope it is to plant trees and shrubs as accents in perennial beds, and to put them in first. It's the best way, really. Woodies are comparatively slow-growing, and this gives them time to come up to size a little before we work other plants around them. I did not do much of this originally, because of the large amount of existing woody material that was here; I found it hard to believe I would ever have room for more trees. Now it is different. I have lost many large trees and developed every border and many garden sites within the lawn. When I plan a new garden area now, I always begin with proportionate woody material. This way, the gardens have "presence" even in the dead of winter. Never feel it is too late or you are too old to remodel an area and put in a tree or a good shrub. They grow fast. I am not young, and as I renovate the borders I have been adding woodies steadily, some in new areas and some to my older plantings. They are very satisfying even as infant things, and each year they grow into their settings, altering the whole scene as they change, with almost magical effect.

Plant big things first because—if for no other reason—when you wait until you have set out bulbs and more delicate plants before digging holes for the big ones, you will inevitably cut into and dig up some of them. Of course, the best reason for establishing the big plants first satisfies a very important principle of design, upon which we have already touched—create the bones, so to speak, of your garden first: establish your tallest point, then some moderately tall points, and lay in the bulky ones around them.

Only a modest amount of imagination is needed to "see" a plant at its mature size in your space and to use this size and shape in your plans. While waiting for an accent plant to reach its full size, you may surround it with hostas or other plants that will be easy to move later on but provide satisfactory bulk in the interim.

In selecting trees and shrubs, as with all plants, it is vitally important to ascertain the degree of sun, shade, and moisture tolerance for each variety and of course the cold tolerance. I would also caution you to go easy on fertilizers and amendments in tree-planting holes. Never exceed the amount of fertilizer recommended by your grower, and keep fertilizers well away from the rootball, if you use them at all. I believe I have better luck with no added fertilizer and with no peat moss or other amendments in the hole, unless I have nothing but straight subsoil to plant in, which I often do; a deep hole is nothing but a water reservoir in my garden.

Planting Bare-Root

In planting bare-root shrubs or trees, dig a wide but shallow hole, not much deeper than the root depth, and loosen three or four inches at the bottom of the hole. Set the plant at its proper depth in the prepared hole, add enough topsoil to stabilize it in position, add water until it sinks away, then pile in more topsoil around the roots, adding composted manure to the soil for the top layer. Press this firmly into place, then water again. You should raise a low mound around the new planting, in which you will leave a shallow bowl for watering. No matter when the tree or shrub is planted, it is good to mulch deeply around the perimeter with compost or shredded bark after watering in. This serves to conserve moisture. Again: if any fertilizer is used, it goes in deep holes out at the drip line, or a bit farther.

Planting a Wrapped Rootball

In plants with a burlap-covered rootball, the grower has usually cut the largest roots quite short, so there should be no problem with strangling growth, though I insist you remove, or at least deeply slash, the burlap after planting. I do not hold with planting burlap and all, let alone plunking in those papier-mâché pots whole! It is handy to leave the burlap on while maneuvering the plant, because it protects the roots, but ropes or wires should be removed entirely and the burlap opened and pulled free after the plant is set in the hole, if possible. In rootballs too large to manipulate, it may be better not to disturb the ball. I feel that burlap left in place too easily influences soft new roots to grow around and around a rootball, choking off growth.

Planting a Potted Woody

Large potted woodies should be unpotted and the roots soaked free, in spite of all you have heard about decomposable papier-mâché pots. Lose the pot. It is not enough, in fact, to simply take plants out of a pot; usually these plants have been growing long enough in their confinement that roots have already begun to grow horizontally around and around the perimeter. If these are not cut or pulled away, the plant will strangle itself as it grows. With larger roots, tease them out and lay the longer ones out in the hole, after cleanly snipping off weak root ends and wounded bits. For potted plants with finer roots, use a sharp knife and slice down shallowly on four sides, top to bottom, presenting some cut edges to promote rooting. The tree-fertilizer plugs often given when one buys trees at a nursery may be set about a foot deep at the extreme outer edges of the hole, where rootlets have to grow a few inches to reach them.

Plant Enough but Avoid Overkill

Consider planting at least a few small trees, even if you have forest giants in the neighborhood. Despite a limited or shady space, small trees or large shrubs form beautiful focal points. In sun, they create small oases of comfort for delicate plants.

Think tall, even for a comparatively small garden, but do not load in too many large trees and shrubs. Leave room for smaller, complementary things to balance the groupings. Be very sure you know the height and bulk at maturity of whatever you plant. Remember—it's necessary to set large specimens as far apart as the full spread of their branches, but smaller woodies may be fitted within that spread according to their comparative size.

My Favorite Small Trees

One of the first trees I wanted in this garden was a Japanese maple. I chose *Acer palmatum* 'Bloodgood', a lovely cutleaf form, and it has done very well here in spite of supposedly being only marginally hardy. Now some eight feet tall and as wide, it has come through many winters without damage. I attribute this to its being located in the north shade of the house but under open sky. The worst killer of tender trees is the freeze-thaw, freeze-thaw of an open situation. When roots stay safely frozen all winter and thaw slowly in spring, they are happy. I protected the young branches the first couple of winters by wrapping the tree in burlap held by clothespins, but now it is on its own.

The new leaves of this tree are such a rich ruby red that they light up the garden behind the screened porch in the spring. It is exciting to see the blue carpet of wood phlox underneath this glowing red. The clear red color is seen all summer on branch tips, while the mature leaves soften in color to a hazy rose-green.

These are trees sensitive to pruning, and I do not touch them except with clean, scrubbed, sharp pruners. I think these trees look best if pruned slightly asymetrically, open in the center and reaching out horizontally and low, with open arms, as in a Japanese painting. The way mine had been prepruned made its growth bunch up in the center and form

a ball-like head. Very young trees may be shaped a little, but it is better to not be too aggressive their first year; it was three years before I dared remove enough wood to really shape this tree. Now I can keep at it every year, removing soft growth and maintaining the form.

The brilliant red-orange berries of *Sorbus alnifolia*, a Korean mountain ash, hang heavily in the sun over my mailbox every fall, and I thoroughly enjoy setting them off with goldenrod and tall hot pink and purple asters for a happy cacophony of color at that time of year. I have just added the late-blooming daylily *Hemerocallis* 'Rocket City' with flowers of the same hot orange as the berries that hang above, so next year's show will be better than ever. Never does a clutter of berries collect on the ground under these trees. Sometime in October every year, the waxwings come in a crowd and clean up the clusters on the branches in one busy day.

The weight of the fruit on this tree sometimes makes it necessary to prune some of it; no matter, the berries make wonderful additions to green arrangements in the house. I also watch the body of the tree, as sometimes branches grow up into the center, where they spoil the shape. I cut these close to the base with sharp pruners, slanting the cuts so no water can rot the open wood.

The Perfect White Accent Tree

A small, bright white-variegated arctic willow shrub, *Salix integra* 'Hakuro Nishiki', is now available either in its original form or as a grafted head on a slender trunk. I have one that is grafted to a six-foot stem, and its branches are tipped all summer long with white, new leaves, slightly curly, with a few peach-colored areas, while the older inner leaves turn green. This coloration gives the effect of blossoms. The fact that this shrub-tree likes afternoon shade gives me the chance to use it where I need a small light. It glows, espe-

cially in the filtered rays of the afternoon sun. When it matures, I can look for a head five or six feet wide. I will prune its branches to keep the top full. To set it off, I put a natural, dwarf, matching tree at the head of the waterfall above the pond. The willows form a remarkable genus, with varieties for every kind of gardener; yes, even the rock gardener, who can find many prostrate alpine willows to suit smaller areas. Many of those listed in good catalogs are suitable to Zones 5 to 3, and the small ones do not have the invasive root systems of our local *Salix nigra*. There are small willows with blue, silver, purple, white, or yellow variegated leaves, and even a few with pink-and-white variegations. This is an underused genus.

Willows need to be cut back, especially the smaller, decorative forms. The best time to shape these trees is in fall, as branches grow back too vigorously during the growing season.

Left: *Salix integra* **'Hakuro Nishiki' is an arctic willow, a shrub only a few feet tall, with clear white variegation. This spectacular cultivar was developed and grafted to a taller trunk in Japan, giving us an incredibly graceful small tree to light up our gardens. This is a sun-grower, though some shade during the day is helpful in keeping the color fresh.**

The six-foot fronds of our native Solomon's seal and an elderberry shrub form a sympathetic background for this showy little tree.

Opposite: A Tiffany glass window might do justice to the glow of spring light in the shade garden as the woods begin to bloom in May. The translucent young leaves of the Japanese maple glow against the background trees and bark paths. Unfurling ferns, sweet woodruff, daffodils, and Virginia bluebells stud the ground, transforming the brown earth into an enchanted glen.

There may be many reasons not to plant the paper bark birch in our cities, but there was a clump here when I came to this house, and I have made the most of it. Because this clump is in the middle of a lawn area surrounded by gardens, I keep the bed long and oval, with simple, uncomplicated plantings of white-variegated hostas and the white-flowering *Daphne axiliflora*.

This daphne is so fragrant in June that I never, ever, pass it without recalling a bit of *The Rubáiyát*: "...such a snare Of perfume shall fling out upon the air As not a true believer passing by But shall be overtaken, unaware."

And when I pass by it in October—surprise! It has put out tiny new blossom bits with wisps of its heady scent, and I must lean close to be overtaken.

A Not-So-Perfect Choice

Betula papyrifera, the paper-barked birch tree, is so ubiquitous in Wisconsin lawns that one would think there was an unwritten law to include at least one in every planting. There was a clump in my front yard when we arrived, and it is still there, thanks to constant monitoring. It has developed a third trunk from its rootstock, having had only two when I first saw it. It has been plagued by disease and beetles, but is currently responding well to the care of a tree service. Yet I don't know how much it really adds to the view; the trunks are awkward, leaning out and over the curb, and they are too tall, pushing up twenty feet into the branches of a burr oak. I like the white trunks, though, as a foil for the fragrant *Daphne axilliflora* and the crisp green and white-edged hostas planted in a long oval bed beneath them, and for the white narcissus that comes earlier. Still, if you haven't gotten a paper birch, I say don't. They are not really happy down here on the flatlands of southern Wisconsin, tending to dry out. They are short-lived and plagued by the bronze birch-borer.

There are other birches—for instance *Betula nigra*, the river birch—that seem resistant to the borer. That variety is much happier and healthier here than the paper bark birch, and it has gorgeous pale but warm-toned peeling bark.

Purple for Contrast

I like some deep-toned foliage here and there, and *Cotinus coggygria* 'Royal Purple', purple smoke bush, gives that incomparable depth to a planting that only the really dark purples can give. I wish I had a place for it in more sun; mine gets only about five hours a day. It is sensitive to cold and freezes back every year, but not all the way, always leaving a substantial shrub of clean, oval leaves. I feel it is gradually building a framework of hardier branches, though it has not as yet sent out its big, smoky plumes for me. The great quilted leaves of *Hosta* 'Sum and Substance' lead one's eye back to this garden spot, where I have set several golden-variegated hostas to keep it company: 'Gold Standard', 'Great Expectations', 'Moonglow', and 'Gold Drop'.

Flowering Trees

While we generally think of flowering trees in full sun, there are many small-sized trees that thrive, and blossom, in various degrees of shade. Check the specifications at the nursery for those you consider for your site. Understory trees can bloom—and can go a long way toward setting their fruit—before the overhead canopy fills out to occlude the sun. Therefore they are in bloom at the same time as spring ephemerals and early bulbs. I have set several kinds carefully where they can be seen from my windows, in company with daffodils, Virginia bluebells, and bloodroot. Even those trees preferring full sun do very well with half-sun or more, if the shade is high and light.

One Good Flowering Crab

Many of the *Malus*, or apple, family are now hybridized for disease resistance, and make wonderful choices for sunny sites. Many are also bred to hold their fruit throughout the winter, when it is taken by birds. This has been a big consideration for those who do not like to clean up yard waste (and that's all of us). There is a rich variety of good, clean flowering crabapple trees now for the homeowner. I planted only one.

In the southwest, mostly sunny, corner garden at the front of our lot, I set the small grafted flowering crab *Malus* 'Coralburst'. It will remain fairly small and its branches will always begin four or five feet from the ground. The branches are horizontal and upcurving, like parasol ribs inside-out, so that surrounding flowering plants have room to grow beneath them. Their buds are a brilliant coral red, and their rather small flowers open white inside with a rosy cast. The fruit is small and bright red, staying on the tree all winter, until taken by birds in their withered state in early spring. It is a real consideration with *Malus* to not only obtain disease-resistant cultivars, but also buy those that hold their fruit and do not create a mess. Such information is readily available when you purchase a tree.

This is not a tree that produces many water sprouts, but I keep an eye open for them on the trunk or rising at an odd angle into the shapely top. I clip them when I see them any time of year.

The Star of Flowering Trees

My greatest delight has been *Chionanthus virginicus*, the silver fringe tree. Every spring, the branches of this small tree are hung with long, irregular, snowy-white, fringelike petals before ever a leaf is seen, though the big leaves begin to appear before the flowers drop. Underplanted with snowdrops and white crocuses, this marvel stands beside the wide brick walk, in a fairly sunny corner behind one of the flat, gray-black split rocks I favor. With its compact shape and big leaves, it is a lovely companion to the Siberian irises, astilbes, hemerocallis, and peonies, which come along later in the summer. It grows to about ten to fifteen feet, and I will certainly have to remove and rearrange plantings because of it eventually, but it will always be a welcome presence.

A Chestnut for the Border

I recently planted *Aesculus parviflora*, the bottlebrush buckeye, far back in the northeast border corner, where it will not show for many years. Because of new diseases these days, some oaks have short lives, and if I should lose some of the large ones in that corner, this buckeye will still provide a lovely backdrop for my borders.

This tree has always attracted me with its marvelous shape, wider at about fifteen feet than it is high, and with a blossom habit that is handsome in the extreme, with foot-tall white candles on all the branches. These come in late summer when no other tree is in bloom. I have seen a red one, *A. x carnea*, blooming in Missouri in understory conditions. It is listed as a Zone 5 tree, which I could probably grow, but I think the white will be more attractive here, as it will light up a dark back corner.

Cherry Trees in Shade

I have two young *Prunus tomentosa*, Nanking cherry, planted in more than half-shade, and they bloom a sight in May, with white-to-pink fuzzy blossoms among creased and pinked leaves. This tree will form a many-stemmed shrub about six to ten feet tall. I keep mine to just a few trunks. Their fruit, they say, is sweet, but you would have to ask the birds. I do not net my fruiting trees.

"Southern-Style" Dogwoods Too

It is no longer necessary to do without the large-flowering dogwoods here in the north. There are, in fact, a bewildering number of *Cornus* cultivars from which to choose.

Cornus kousa chinensis, the Chinese dogwood, has given us an option of "flowers" (actually petal-like bracts around small central bosses of flowers) like those of *C. florida*, along with hardiness to at least Zone 5. These trees survive and bloom here because their blossoms come along in June, long after all danger of frost is past. They are not foolproof, but they do well if protected for the first few winters. There are several pink-flowering cultivars, probably a bit less hardy than the white-flowering form, and there is also a white-variegated dogwood, *C. controversa* 'Variegata', one of which I have just brought through its first winter. The leaf variegation is brilliant, with some snow-white leaves, and I look forward to enjoying its effect against dark green background trees. Several growers are experimenting with hardiness, leaf color, and blossom habit, so look for more kinds of beautiful *Cornus* to be available for Zone 4. Right now the lowest listing for *kousa* cultivars is Zone 5, but we must be brave and try them.

The Hardy Silverbells

Halesia carolinia, or Carolina silverbell, is a perfectly lovely small tree for the edge of the woods. It is a stunning sight in May when every reaching branch is hung with one-inch shallow bells, white or pink, depending on the cultivar. All the flowers seem to fall at once after a week or ten days, covering the ground with a carpet of color. My experience with this cultivar, however, indicates that the soil must have a neutral to slightly acid situation, or the leaves become chlorotic. This happened to mine, and although it didn't affect the bloom, it did cause me worry. One application of sulfur took about six months to be effective, but it corrected the situation, and I watch the tree carefully. My tree grows about eight feet from a giant bur oak and thrives under its branches.

Opposite: The June show put on by *Chionanthus virginicus*, the silver fringe tree, is unexcelled, in my estimation. This very young specimen blooms at one corner of my entrance garden behind a flat rock. It has been pruned up slightly to allow light to reach plants around its feet, but it will naturally be casting more shade as it grows. We must allow for change in the garden, so as this tree gets larger I will alter the plantings to suit. For now, I simply enjoy the combinations each season as they happen and do what I must, or what I wish, to enhance them as they change.

Redbuds for the North

Cercis canadensis, or redbud, is happy in an understory setting in our climate if it gets close to a half-day or more of sun and is in a somewhat protected location. This tree is somewhat tricky to start, however; I tried one a few years ago and killed it with kindness. I put in the "obligatory" packets of fertilizer and set the tree carefully in a mulched hole with copious amendments. I watered it, mulched it, and babied it. It grew like crazy, and I was sure it would bloom the next spring. What it did is promptly die. Redbuds need a tough start. Don't coddle them. Put them in a shallow loosened bed of your lawn soil, dug wide, and if you use the fertilizer packets, bury them at the extreme outer edges, spacing them widely around the trunk. I have another redbud now that I bought for just a few dollars when it was about one foot tall, and I set it out on a slope not too far from the silver bells tree. I planted it hastily, in plain soil. It was hidden from view, so I never fertilized it, and forgot it. It grew to a wand with big heart-shaped leaves in a year or two, and I forgot it again. It grew to a fish-pole-sized arch with even bigger leaves. Finally, I had to shape it, realizing that one long tail of tree was going to flop over the west side of the fern garden forever if I didn't do something. (Since that time, I have learned that it is proper not to prune brand-new trees until they have had one or two seasons of growth.) It's quite nicely shaped now, and when it bloomed last spring it made a lovely addition to the background of that border. I was encouraged by its success to set out a many-stemmed specimen on the back slope in half-shade last spring, where it also has prospered mightily, forming many long, graceful stems.

Magnolias That Bloom for Us

Several of the smaller magnolia varieties will grow here and thrive in less than a full day of sun, if they are under

Left: I think 'Betty' is even prettier in her coat of glossy leaves, with little arrangements of bloom and bud happening off and on all summer and fall, until frost. She reminds me to look up.

Opposite: *Magnolia* 'Betty' in her May bloom is a beacon in the landscape. She is best in the mid-background, with bulb beds at her feet and budding trees above and behind.

open sky. My small *Magnolia* 'Betty' is set between the neighbor's house on the east and our house on the west, and the houses are close enough together that the tree is in shade until after noon, and back in the shade by about four o'clock —but it has open sky above. It makes a bouquet of itself in May, with deep rose straplike petals four inches long before the leaves come, unless the frost gets the buds. After it is in full, glossy leaf, it keeps putting out posies of its buds and blooms, off and on, all summer long. It is approximately eight feet tall now, about its full height, with only two or three trunks.

Magnolia 'Elizabeth' has been tempting me these last few seasons as I see its clear yellow blossoms in the catalogs, and I might succumb next spring, perhaps setting it to the north of the great white shrub rose at the bottom of my driveway garden, where it would form a stunning backdrop. *Magnolia stellata* is another form I always admire in Wisconsin gardens, as it survives even at curbside, putting out its white stars early in the spring and remaining petite in the landscape.

The blooming branches of pagoda dogwood form a tiered canopy over a back corner planted with some of my commonest plants, reminding me that it is not necessary to purchase dozens of high-priced hostas in order to create a stunning effect in shade. With the dogwood overhead and the ostrich ferns behind, even plain old *Hosta fortunei* "Aureo-marginata" is fresh and bright in this almost neglected corner. Any white accent added, such as the *Lamium* 'White Nancy', tends to maximize the effect of these common plants.

If you have been ignoring a long, straight row of old hostas somewhere in the sun, you are doing them an injustice. They are ready and willing to perform this kind of magic for you, if you open your eyes.

Native Trees That Flower

Our native dogwoods have a very different bloom habit from that of the varieties *florida* and *kousa*, and of course they are hardy to Zone 4 at least. They have flat racemes of fuzzy, fragrant, white flowers. *Cornus alternifolia* 'Pagoda Dogwood' and *C. racemosa (paniculata)*, gray dogwood, were present on my lot when I arrived, and plentiful in the second growth woodland next door. They can put up with the worst of our winters. I have lots of both because they are fairly small. Pagoda is my favorite. Its flat racemes of blossoms in spring scent the area delicately and sweetly, and the black berries on their red stems are beautiful in the fall when the leaves turn crimson and purple. Birds love the fruit. I was able to pull up many small Pagoda seedlings from a neighboring lot about to be torn up by bulldozers several years ago, and all have grown into nice small trees, the largest about ten feet tall and

somewhat wider in branch spread. Horizontal in habit, Pagoda spreads its arms low and wide. I like the way the lower branches can sweep the ground like skirts, but I prune them up a few feet by taking off the downward-growing branches, thereby letting the primroses and trilliums show. The leaves are attractive all summer, being set in irregular fans, shining and fatly veined. I try to keep the growth low and horizontal by cutting out water sprouts with a long-handled pruner. They sprout higher and higher as the tree grows, straight up from the top branches. Dogwoods are worth the work, but a caution is necessary: these trees need good disease control. I have lost several because neighbors did not control the spread of some blight, and where they touched mine over the back fence, mine were destroyed before I noticed. Good housekeeping keeps them clean: cutting off blighted branches cleanly, disposing of them in trash bags, and cleaning the pruners between every job.

The gray dogwoods have a similar blossom habit, but duller leaves. They are a bit more trouble, and not as pretty in summer, but their white fruits on red stems set themselves off so nicely against a woodsy background in winter that I protect them and do the necessary frequent pruning. Both kinds have water sprouts and suckers, and the grays will make dense clumps if not tended. I like to arborize such shrub-trees, cutting out new suckers and forming one or two trunks, because space is precious, and I have so many things I want to grow underneath them.

Amelanchiers are also native trees, and a good wood's-edge choice. Shadblow, Juneberry, and serviceberry are just a few of their nicknames. They come in many named cultivars and are extremely hardy. Their flowers are small, white, fragrant racemes in spring, and their fruit is a richer, sweeter version of the blueberry. Try to beat the birds to at least one bowlful, or enough to add to your cornflakes! In fall, all of these small trees turn bright colors, coral to gold. They take quite a lot of sun but adapt nicely to the understory or an edge of woods, in either tree or shrub form.

Hamamelis, or witch hazel, is also a natural choice for woodland landscapes, being native to the Midwest, and it has lovely, distinctive blooms. I chose *Hamamelis virginiana*, which makes a nice small tree, but it blooms in November under its big leaves, where I never see the thread-petalled yellow flowers. Early spring-blooming cultivars are just as hardy, and their odd yellow or orange blossoms studding the knobby stems are very fragrant and—best of all—visible. I am considering several more to form a thicket around 'Virginia'.

I have a small *Aronia arbutifolia* 'Brilliantissima', or chokeberry, another native tree-shrub, which fills in the end of a long border. It is surrounded by *Matteuccia pennsylvanica* (now called *Pteritis nodulosa*), ostrich fern. The chokeberry blooms with smaller versions of the Pagoda white doilies and produces black berries that the birds eat, but I love it most of all for its scarlet fall color.

Small Conifers

I have only just begun to use small conifers as garden plants, though I have always admired them. In public gardens I have seen combinations of conifers with only mosses or thymes as underplanting, and they are breathtaking. My style of gardening, and my need for so many kinds of plants, precludes this treatment, but I encourage you to look into it. A raised bed with stone outcroppings and a composition of these miniature trees can be the focal point of anyone's landscaping. This takes a certain restraint I lack, that's all; in limited space, it is difficult for me to give up any sizable area to one kind of thing. My need to have more kinds of plants is just too strong.

I increasingly appreciate dwarf conifers as companion plants, although the cultivars I have used with success are few. The stiff clay of our soil discourages their roots. Now that I have learned to import good soils and make raised beds, I am experimenting with at least one new conifer each year.

Picea orientalis 'Aurea' is a delicate little golden spruce, one that holds its pencil-thin branches nicely over a floriferous berm in my garden, and its golden spring color adds to the effect, especially when the small bulbs are in bloom. It is about four feet tall at this point, and a see-through little tree, so it does not obscure the slender stems and small flowers of species narcissus, nor does it look out of proportion to the *Viola labradorica* carpeting the ground beneath it. This is not a dwarf; it will top out at ten or fifteen feet in perhaps twenty-five years. I feel it will enhance its setting as well or better at full size, since it is of such delicate texture.

A fat little blue spruce cultivar, *Picea pungens* 'Montgomery', sits firmly on a gravelly berm near the curb, in the most sun I can provide, and it is a real complement to the alpine plants that surround it. Right now it is not a foot high yet spreads about a foot and a half, though it will attain a height of three to five feet in time. Lots of time, I hope. Oh, well, I can enlarge that garden—let's see: another yard or so of scree mix, a couple of extra-large rocks, some added height, and a few more rock plants for the shade!

An Irish juniper, *Juniperus communis* 'Hibernica', makes a dark, slender column about four feet tall, standing like a small sentinel nearly at the eastern end of the gravel berm. This beauty is only about a foot and a half wide. When its growing tips are pale and tender in the spring, I nip them all the way up and at the peak to keep the juniper's shape and somewhat limit its growth, although where I have it, it will look well at twice its size, which it will not attain for another ten or fifteen years.

J. squamata 'Blue Star' is set nearby, where its very small,

Top: Picea orientalis 'Aurea', a fragile-appearing golden spruce, is a lovely sight in bud. Always delicate, the slender branches of needles are tipped with golden new growth in spring, gradually darkening in summer, but never becoming dense.

It is planted on the ridge of the front berm to provide a year-round presence and light shade for the northern slope that faces the house, and to accompany the mostly small perennials that appear in summer.

Bottom: Picea pungens **'Montgomery'** creates a good spruce-blue accent in the pastel and silver setting of the gritty berm. This excellent dwarf tree was planted deeply into the upside-down clumps of sod taken from the lawn, which were left for a year or two to decompose under about a foot of the sandy grit. The tree has never had a brown needle. 'Montgomery' will grow to perhaps five feet tall and as wide, and I will simply change the garden to go along with its changing size.

flat, blue shape is a perfect foil for spiky crocosmias, with their red wings. It is less than a foot wide, and only a few inches high. Its flattened bluish needles are really starry-shaped and glisten with a light varnish against the pebbles. This beauty will spread slowly to cover much more space, but it is a true dwarf and will never rise above a foot tall.

All of these evergreen gems love the good drainage of the sharp sand-gravel mixture of this berm. They are especially attractive in that garden right now because of the stony soil and the small size of the surrounding alpine plants, which put the little conifers into the place of trees in a miniature mountain landscape. A gardener changes perspective as things grow, and I will rethink the plantings around the little conifers as they need revision.

Pinus mugo, if kept debudded to control height, is a perfect accent tree, especially, I think, at the near end of a berm, where its bushy, long-needled form properly terminates the planting. If I did not remove all its candles, it would soon be much too hearty and tall, so every spring when the new bud candles on top are about an inch long, I pinch them all. Beneath it, on the shady side, I have left a flat bed for tiny spring irises, both *Iris pumila* and *cristata*. On the sunny side, wooly thyme is trying to hold its own against *Geranium sanguineum* 'John Elsley', which spreads its red-green leaves and deep carmine little blossoms wider and wider all summer. Still prettier with it are the *Allium senescens* 'Glaucum' on the driveway side, where their blue foliage sets off the dark pine, and the many small globes of rose blossom finish the picture in late summer.

A Few Choice Flowering Shrubs

There is a bush clematis, *Clematis heracleifolia davidiana*, which grows in sparse gritty soil for me. I do not fertilize it. It is enhanced in late summer by rich blue blossoms tightly ringed around the leaf axils of the upper third of its stems. Individual blooms are an inch or less in diameter but cluster thickly together, and their fragrance reaches away into the street, causing visitors to look around for a big, flowering tree. This plant thoroughly enjoys the good drainage and chancy watering of the gravelly berm, though its roots, I am sure, go well down into lawn soil underneath. It is a sprawler, however, and I can only hope the poor rations of water and a no-fertilization regimen will keep it close it to its present size and shape, which I like.

Fothergilla gardenii is a small shrub that should be used much more in this climate. It might take full sun—I am not sure—but it does very well with a half-day or so in my garden. It is located near the front porch in fairly heavy clay soil, which gives me the impression that it is undemanding, even though the catalogs say it likes acid humus. I treat it to manure mulches and put all my coffee grounds around its roots, but otherwise leave it to its own resources. In spring, it has vanilla-scented white bottlebrush flowers, which last for two weeks or more. By the first of October it begins to turn, one leaf at a time, to soft red-coral, and it remains a fall feature of the garden until brisk winds carry away the small leaves. More sun will give it more intense fall color.

Daphnes have a scent that, once experienced, is never forgotten, and seems to have a most nostalgic power. A *Daphne axiliflora* was given to me by a friend several years ago. There are many offsets all around it every year that would grow into a thicket if I did not share them with friends. It is a welcome presence in light woods and semi-shady borders.

A *D. x burkwoodii* 'Carol Mackie' now shares the shady berm with other special plants. I attempted to order this variegated form from different suppliers for three or four years, without success, before finally finding one at a local nursery.

Its firm, slender, oval leaves are crisply edged in gold, turning to white as the season advances. This daphne needs afternoon shade, a well-built, light, loamy soil, good drainage, and careful mulching to hold moisture and prevent winter heaving. A winter protection of light evergreen boughs or straw will help bring it through the winter.

Creating an Artificial Environment

The rhododendrons and azaleas we love to see in the Blue Ridge are quite possible to grow up here, but for me to have them survive it is necessary to create an artificially acid environment and give them excellent drainage. Peat moss is the best answer. These shrubs like a very wide planting hole, and if your soil is dense and heavy, they will thrive if you plant them in a mound of peat and chopped leaf mulch well above the soil line. Set them shallowly on this mound, leaving a saucer to hold moisture so it can slowly seep down through the roots and drain away.

I planted one *Rhododendron* 'PJM' years ago and followed the directions carefully. I now have a great six-foot shrub spreading at least as wide. It is semi-evergreen, with some leaves staying on the plant all winter. This cultivar was bred at the Weston Nursery in Massachusetts and had spent one winter outdoors in its gallon can, so I knew it would be hardy if I did as directed. It grows in a peaty bed at the top of a deep berm on the north side of the house, with open sky above. I add about a soup can full of powdered garden sulfur annually around the drip line, and stir it into the soil slightly. The buds form by October, and in May the plant is covered totally with bright lavender blossoms. I do not happen to think, as some gardeners do, that this is an unpleasant or difficult color. I just give it bright red tulips as companions! If you really hate magenta, 'PJM' has many new cultivars these days, with the same requirements but differ-

ent-colored blossoms: 'Olga Mezzitt' is a pure pink, 'Aglow' is pink, and 'Balta' is snowy white.

Rhododendrons and azaleas prefer lots of light but no exposure to hot, direct afternoon sun. Both are understory shrubs and therefore happy in high shade, especially in more southern sites. They will actually thrive in nearly full sun in our zone; give them an east or north exposure, shelter from the late afternoon glare, and follow the directions for planting in peat moss and acidifying, and you will be able to grow and enjoy them. Azaleas are deciduous, losing their leaves and setting their flower buds in fall. The azaleas recommended most for this climate come from a University of Minnesota project and are called the Northern Lights series. *Rdododendron* 'Northern Lights', 'Golden Lights', 'White Lights', and 'Rosy Lights' are self-explanatory names for varieties providing highly satisfactory color in spring, just as *R.* 'PJM' is fading. They are all fragrant.

Some Large Shrubs

Almost treelike if arborized and controlled, the native *Sambucus canadensis*, or elderberry, can be a handsome presence in summer with its wide, lacy, scented bloom, and in fall with black fruit. If it is not controlled, it is a jumbled, leggy, suckery thing that has little value in the landscape except when the blossoms come.

It would love full sun but has done very well for me in about half-shade. I have had one grow eight feet tall with a spread of ten feet, making huge plates of blossom and arching over a regular cave of undergrowth to create the loveliest spot in the garden. I arborized it by cutting it back to a few main trunks and keeping suckers and water sprouts out. It provided a charming and amusing sideshow every year as its tiny blossoms fell, like scalloped white sequins with a minuscule hole in the center of each, into the dark fishpond. Alas,

the arbor was heavily infested with aphids one year and died out enough that it had to be cut back. The new suckers now developing have already blossomed, and next season I will have a beautiful show. Sambucus as an ornamental is inclined to sucker horribly, but it is easy to take out the water sprouts, which can be cut at any time during the growing season.

The *S. canadensis* has been used as food and medicine for centuries. The blossoms and berries are healthful and delicious as food, and tinctures and teas of the flowers, leaves, roots, and bark are used for many purposes, particularly against colds and flu. The mild, fragrant tea made from distilled water and elder blossom is delicious on ice with honey, and it is also a most effective skin freshener.

I do not recommend using any of the other cultivars of

Left: This rather early view of the back garden features a large native *Sambucus canadensis*, our native elderberry, at its most beautiful. This variety has edible black berries, good for making jelly, sauce, or wine, but it is the blossoms that make it worthwhile to cultivate. Elderberry shrubs are always attractive, unless one lets them get overgrown with suckers and water sprouts, which they will readily do. The flower heads do not have an ugly, brown stage, but go seamlessly from white pearls to white fluff to green beads to black berries, and their falling petals are like tiny white sequins.

Opposite: The magenta-pink of *Rhododendron* 'PJM' is set off beautifully, in my eyes, by the red of *Tulipa greiggii* 'Red Riding Hood', and the yellow and white daffodils. This is the most cheerful of spring combinations, made even more enjoyable by its placement beside the screened porch, where we can see it while having lunch or tea.

Top: When the elderberry heads are still partly in their seed-pearl bud stage, but mostly open, I always cut a few for breakfast. Leaving a stem about an inch long for handling, I rinse carefully to eliminate any unwelcome creatures, and dry the whole blossom heads upside-down on paper towels. I whip up a fritter batter of eggs and water, with a shake of flour, in a pie tin, and dip the flat heads one at a time. I fry them in butter and serve with warm maple syrup. The taste is exquisite, something between French toast and elder-flower perfume. I did not invent this dish; it originated in Europe, possibly from Bavaria.

Bottom: *Sambucus canadensis* 'Aurea' is a golden-chartreuse eldeberry presence in the spring garden, with soft rusty-rose tints at the tips of its growing stems. Because it sheds a light that is needed in the shady north garden, I grow it in possibly less sun than it would like. This one is doing well in about half shade.

Blossom and fruit are earlier than those of *S. canadensis*, and not good to eat.

Sambucus as food; at least one of them, *S. racemosa* 'Plumosa Aurea', is purported to be toxic, lovely as it is. With its chartreuse leaves cut into fancy patterns, my specimen is beautiful in part shade, though I think it would like more sun. It was three years old before it bloomed, produced its red berries, and stood straight and grew strong vertical trunks, but it is now a substantial shrub.

I have another elder which may be toxic; it is *S. pubens*, an American native. I admired these in a friend's border, and one has now come to live here. Its white blossoms come so early that the berries are present in July, and they are red. It makes a tall, rather woodier plant than the other varieties, with bigger leaves, and it formed substantial bushes for my friend. In her border, however, they were abominably cut, with hedge shears, in a vertical fashion, so that the branches were unnaturally even and had a thick brush at the tips, not at all the way I like to see them. My plant is being shaped in a more open style, which means having only a few of the older central canes removed all the way to the ground every year, and only a few of the outer branches judiciously shortened. It has room to become a good large presence at the north foot of one of the green woodland islands.

There are chocolate- and purple-leaved varieties of *Sambucus,* notably *S. nigra* 'Guincho Purple', which has deep purple leaves and pink flowers. I am eager to try it, but that would demand a major rethinking of my spaces. Perhaps it is time.

Some Old Standbys

In my grandmother's day, every house in the Midwest seemed to have hydrangea bushes in their front yards. These are seldom seen now except in cemeteries. We cannot grow the blue ones, or indeed any of the highly colored varieties, in this climate, especially with our neutral soil.

The only hydrangea I have tried to grow is the oak-leaved variety *Hydrangea quercifolia* 'Snow Queen', which has not done as well as I'd hoped. The shrub is probably four years old now, and it just bloomed for the first time after an unusually mild winter. I know I am pushing the envelope of hardiness for this variety a bit far. It usually freezes back just enough each winter to need all its energy to simply grow the following season. I protect it in winter with burlap wrapped around hinged plant stakes, unfolded only halfway and set to form a square large enough not to crowd the branches. I don't do this for too many plants. I am willing to put forth some effort for the huge conical white blooms, which change from white to rose to bronze-brown in late summer—a gorgeous effect that forms the perfect focal point for a woods-edge garden. The bronzy fall color of the leaves is lovely too. I will hate it if I have to remove this good shrub, but if a cold winter takes it down again, I will have no choice.

The Peegee hydrangea, *H. paniculata* 'Grandiflora', is a good Zone 4 choice for reliable foliage and flowers, but I believe it needs more sun than *H. quercifolia*. These are best used like small trees—as specimens—where their upright conical white flowers can show fully. I have not grown this variety, but I like its form, which is like a small tree.

Viburnum is another shrub choice I have not exploited to the fullest, though there are deliciously scented ones and gloriously flowered ones, my favorite being the horizontally tiered *Viburnum plicatum tomentosum* 'Mariessii', which is hardy in our zone and tolerant of shade. It grows very large and makes huge lace doilies of horizontal bloom.

I do have many large bushes of *V. trilobum*, the American highbush cranberry, in the back borders. This forms rather helter-skelter tall shrubs in my high shade, and would probably like much more sun. I cut water sprouts and suckers out, and head back long branches, but mine has taken years, and the loss of some tall trees, to look as well as

it does now. The red berries hang on for some time, and when birds take them they drop seed in the woodsy gardens, so I always have a surprise bush here and there.

Caveat Emptor

Beginners often buy too quickly, either because of extravagant claims in catalogs, or through trusting inexperienced (I say that to be kind) salespersons. I bought my highbush cranberries in good faith as shade shrubs more than twenty years ago, when I was less experienced. I also purchased (from the same salesman) *Physocarpus opulifolius*, the eastern ninebark, and planted several in the same shady area, to almost total failure. Such a lovely shrub, too, with clear yellow-green, interesting, pleated foliage. I have no sunnier spot to move them into, and I still see one or two struggling along, with long withes angling off in all directions.

Roses for the Mixed Garden

I leave roses until last, because they are not the stars of my gardens, but merely the background furniture, put in mostly because of bulk and fragrance. I use only very hardy shrub roses, which smell wonderful and gladly share their territory. Hybrid teas require a royal solitude that doesn't fit my style, and they need far too much care in this latitude for the show they give, in my opinion.

The earliest of my shrub roses to bloom is the fragrant white *Rosa* 'Mme. Hardy', which never loses an inch to frost and multiplies its wickedly armed canes every year. It is now over seven feet tall and as wide, even with judicious pruning. I have planted late-blooming white clematis around it, so that when the roses are over their heavy flush of blossom in June I will still have white flowers. I get another smaller flush of roses in mid-July.

All of the other shrub roses lose at least some part of

their canes to the coldest winters and have to be cut down to about two feet, but they all come back and bloom well. *R.* 'Heritage' is the most beautiful of these in bloom, and it flowers quite heavily several times during the season. It is the most delicate pink imaginable, with hundred-petal rounded flowers and darker pink buds, and true old-rose fragrance.

R. rubrifolia, another totally carefree rose, has become quite popular as a landscape planting recently, with its ruddy blue foliage and lovely bright hips. It bears single red flowers. Although *R. rubrifolia* is a rather large, free presence, I have just added one to my difficult dry border along my neighbor's fence, as this hardy rose can manage some dry shade, or so they say. I need it for its bluish leaf coloration and its bulk in this corner, where so many things have petered out for lack of sustenance. Deep blue alpine clematis keeps it company.

The Hardiest Climber

One climbing rose has become quite famous in this northern country for its total hardiness and beauty. It is *R.* 'Henry Kelsey', a part of the Explorer Series developed in Canada, reportedly hardy to Zone 3 and maybe even Zone 2. It has very wide, single, deep red blooms, off and on all summer, and it climbs to ten feet, not needing any pulling down or cutting back, except for shaping, and no cover on the canes. I have two young plants started on the brick south face of the garage at the back of the entrance garden. After their first winter, not one of the rose canes had frozen back, and the plant has produced many long wands, full of the large, single, red blooms. The roses are growing so fast that I have had to get into the garden several times and tie up new waving stems. The wrought iron fan trellises are almost full of vines already.

The more tender climbing *R.* 'America' rises by the front door, where it puts out tea-rose quality blossoms of a beautiful hot coral. Its canes freeze back every spring, sometimes to the ground, but it blooms thickly on a three-foot bushy stand in June and then sends up long canes for occasional buds all summer. But it is in high shade much of the day, even though on a south-facing wall, and that makes it skimpy in its repeat bloom. Last year I planted *Clematis* 'The President' alongside it for a deep purple accent and for foliage that fills the top section of the chain trellis.

My Prescription for Rose Care

As I have said, I concede to poisons only in the case of my roses; black spot is so ugly, and beetle-chewed rosebuds so sad. Once each spring I apply a systemic mixture for chewing insects that includes fertilizer, then once in summer go to a solution of Epsom salts, a half-cup to a gallon of water, as fertilizer. I never fertilize after July. I also throw banana peels under the bushes, and I keep about a two-inch layer of composted manure or shredded bark layered around their feet.

It is impractical for me to treat half-hardy climbing roses as directed, digging the long trenches in my heavy soil and laying down the branches for the winter. I take my climbing 'America' off the wire trellis and lay it gently down, under burlap, but this is as far as I go.

All my roses get only a half-day of sun, but they are under open sky. They bloom extravagantly in June and sporadically all summer, some of them ending up in October with the most beautiful blossoms of all.

Vines

I use clematis vines on trellises and tree stumps in rather the same way I use shrubs, for filler and bulk as well as color. These plants are especially grateful for a well-prepared, wide planting hole, dug deeply and softened with humus. The old

Opposite: *Clematis* 'Nelly Moser' was planted about twenty years ago on the southeast corner of the brick garage wall. I used a bushel of compost. A flat rock was placed over the roots, and a few hostas were planted around it to shade and cool its roots. 'Nelly' reblooms off and on after its great June show.

Right: The mop-heads of clematis after its spectacular bloom give us the quiet green background that sets off the later blooming perennials.

Opposite: *Clematis terniflora (paniculata)* 'Sweet Autumn Clematis' climbs up a skeleton of dead honeysuckle bush, increasing its spread every year, wrapping itself into a young redbud tree and various tall perennials. That habit does no harm to the other plants, because this clematis blooms on new wood, and is therefore cut back to one foot about the middle of March. It is a bit of work to pull off all the long, winding vines from everywhere and clean up the bed, but this is the earliest spring job, and it is good to be out.

PHOTOGRAPHY BY TOM COTTINGTON

Clematis 'Nelly Moser' on the corner of the brick garage wall is so big now that its weight pulls the mortar-bolts out of the wall when the wind whips it on its chain-link trellis. It has been there for twenty years. In June it blooms all the way to the roof, a solid sheet of pale pink, and almost immediately, while it is sending out a veil of new foliage, a new flush of bloom is going on at the original level. I have to cut away a bushel or more of two-foot green foliage just to keep it in bounds and to let the new blooms show. That is the only pruning it gets. I started its roots under a flat rock and set in a hosta at its feet, but otherwise it has sun from morning to midafternoon. I feed it occasionally in early spring, and it has a mulch of rotted leaves.

I like to plant two or more clematis together, and if you want to do this for more continuous bloom, be certain you have the same types together. The spring bloomers should be pruned for shaping only after the bloom period, whereas early summer bloomers may be left alone or pruned six to eight inches after blooming, and late summer-to-fall bloomers must be cut back in March to twelve inches from the ground. I have planted *C. montana rubens* with *C. terniflora (paniculata)* 'Sweet Autumn Clemantis' because both need this severe pruning. *C. montana* has fragrant, anemone-like two-inch pink flowers for a long period in early autumn, so that when the Sweet Autumn bursts into its white clouds in September, pink flowers are still among the white.

As I mentioned, I also plant clematis vines with climbing and shrub roses, which go out of bloom so soon. This way I have the anticipation and enjoyment of fresh bloom that keeps me roaming the garden all season.

The (usually) beautiful white *C.* 'Henryii' is planted near the tall lilacs, but alas, it is suffering from dwarfism because of my dreadful mistake about lime, and it produces only a few small blooms. This season I dug and washed its

roots, took out a bushel of the limey soil, and replaced it with something wonderful. Remember: Do not use lime on your clematis unless you have very acid soil—then do it carefully, once. I know I'll never forget that advice.

I have now begun planting some of the *C. viticella* and *C. alpina* varieties, which do so well on the north side in shade. Some of them make small bell-shaped flowers, from brilliant red-purple through the blue-purples and blues—even yellow! There is a world of color and charm in clematis, and think how little garden space is taken up by these vines, with their skinny ankles. Just give them something to sprawl over, and they are happy, even in quite a bit of shade. My clematis dream is to have many of these small vines clambering over rocks and shrubs around the fish pond in the shade, hanging their delicate pink, white, and purple bells in surprising places. The pond area especially needs vines, as the big boulders along the back side are laid over pond liner, and nothing will grow directly beside them. With the waterfall, the ferns, and the low-growing hostas, vine-covered rocks will make that area into the focus of the entire garden.

A Climbing Shrub?

Hydrangea anomala petiolaris is not a shrub but a clinging vine that needs little help to scramble up a tree or a wall once it gets a good start. I planted one on the west side of a large oak several years ago, which has not bloomed as yet. The requirements for growing these vines are few: good humus, occasional attention to watering, and perhaps tying up tendrils in the early stages. After a year or two the clinging is done by the vine. The leaves and flowers of this vine are nearly identical to shrub hydrangeas; once at the blooming stage, which can take a few years, these vines set wide horizontal platters of lacy white and look their best climbing up a good high vertical.

Grow Beautiful Berries

A vine grows up the wooden framework of my mailbox, which has people ringing my doorbell. It is the beautiful *Ampelopsis brevipedunculata* 'Elegans', a variegated porcelain vine. The leaves of this variety are spattered white on green and shaped somewhat like grape leaves. The vine does blossom, but it is neither the leaves nor the rather inconspicuous blooms that attract so much attention—it is the fruit. In midsummer, small firm berries almost like grapes begin to form from the blossoms. These are pale green, changing gradually to a white jade color and then flushing to turquoise and purple. They arrive in sequence, so that beads of all sizes, up to the maximum of about three-eighths of an inch, and in all the colors, are present together among the lacy leaves. This vine grows in as much sun as I can give anything, which means it has open sky above it but is shaded in the morning and again in the afternoon by tall trees. I never fertilize it, and it grows in a gravelly clay mixture that seems pretty forbidding. Perhaps this is why I still love it; I have heard it is a wild grower and can overwhelm its area quite rapidly if grown in a too-fertile spot. Mine has been in place for five or six years and is still a modest, though thick cover for a damaged mailbox post.

Perennials for Shade

Gardening for pleasure—for the refreshment of the eyes, the body, and the whole being—

began with the domestication of shade. The first pleasure gardens were retreats from the Biblical desert,

inspired by the natural oasis. To the parched mind and body, the oasis was a place of

supernal attraction, a pool of shade, of coolness, and of water. The home garden was

conceived as a private fragment of this luxury of nature.

George Schenk, *The Complete Shade Gardener*, Houghton Mifflin, 1984

ACQUIRING EXCEPTIONAL perennials is in general a lot easier these days than when I began my search. Only recently can we find a good variety, especially in shade plants. Whole nurseries are now devoted to cultivating shade plants and whole catalogs to promoting them; an enormous industry has grown up around their propagation. Shade is no longer a gardening liability but an opportunity. If you have shade, you will be able to grow some of the rarest and most beautiful plants available in this part of the world.

I am often stopped in my tracks near the fish pond in early spring just by the pure sight of tall, yellow-variegated *Iris pseudacorus* 'Variegata' so perfectly placed before half-grown *Cimicifuga ramosa* 'Atropurpurea', not even in bloom, with the great-leaved, crimped-edged pale *Hosta* 'Maekawa' developing at its feet, an *Athyrium nipponicum* 'Pictum', or Japanese painted fern, in front, and a dark clump of velvety *Asarum canadense*, Canadian ginger, in the rocks at the back. Breathtaking. A well-footed planting—though I remember a lot of experimentation before it came right.

The border carried around to the right of that garden is *Hosta* 'Kabitan': little, chartreuse long-rayed stars, which I keep dividing to preserve their open, attractive shape. Small specimen ferns spring from the rock terrace and border all around this small garden. *Iris siberica* 'White Swirl', *Epimedium* (several cultivars), *Lamiastrum galeobdolon* 'Herman's Pride', a young *Hosta* 'Sunpower', a glowing, pale yellow specimen of *H.* 'Janet', and a grand, upright Christmas fern make the whole a lovely picture, without a single blossom. Forget-me-nots, spring bulbs, *Primula japonica*, and an elegant pale blue camassia, or squamash lily, plus the hostas and the cimicifuga itself, when in bloom, give additional transitory beauty, of course, but aren't all necessary.

In other areas, I have set large-leaved plants among ferns and hostas: the wheels of rodgersias and hellebores, the bulk of kirengeshoma, the lift of tall thalictrum, and the spray of astilbes against *Aruncus dioicus*, all nicely faced down by *Pulmonaria* 'British Sterling' and *Lamium* 'White Nancy'. When the primulas bloom and the huge three-part leaves of *Arisaema triphyllum*, our native jack-in-the-pulpit, unfold from their thick purple stems in their voluntary nooks and crannies, I think I couldn't have planned it better. (A lot of it is volunteer growth!)

Analyzing Shade

My garden really has no area where there is not shade for at least a third of the day, and some spots are in dense shade all day. It should be no wonder that it has become my favorite kind of garden. A lot of my gardening experimentation has been done to discover what kind of shade, and how much, each plant requires. All plants need light to grow, of course, it's just that some cannot take much direct sunlight. Often, I must move plants around once or twice before they are happy; it's almost like moving furniture to find the most pleasing arrangement. The catalog designation "P Sh" for "Part Shade" is all one usually gets in the way of plant preferences, and, unfortunately, the words are interpretable in many ways. One type of plant might need all-day shade of the high, dappled variety; others might do better when full shade follows morning sun, or in the north shadow of a building. The latter may seem like constant shade, but if open sky is above, that condition may be treated as part shade. In general, the more light you can give even a shade plant, without exposing it to burning rays, the better the results.

A Picturesque Selection

You will not find alphabetical lists of plants here, but rather, I suppose, a set of mental images of garden beds in their different phases, with plants arranged in compatible

The heavy wands of *Cimicifuga ramosa* 'Atropurpurea' begin to arch downward from their seven-foot height in September as the purple buds open to white fuzzy flowers, bringing them to eye level. The leaves of 'Atropurpurea' are a dark green with purplish undertones, and the stems are a deep, almost black shade of purple. The clumps multiply nicely after the first growing season into six or seven tall stalks, with wide, ferny leaves on the lower half.

The fragrance of these blossoms is pervasive and sweet, but for some reason nearly indescribable. To some, it smells like strong peppermint candy, very sugary; to others, like warm, fresh corn tortillas!

groupings. I give you descriptions of most of the shade-loving plants I like to grow, beginning very roughly with the tallest plants (although some of the smaller varieties seem to just insinuate themselves into the text!) and finishing up with the smallest. I like to use them all, short and tall, in a huge, spreading mix, and I tell you which ones spread, by how much, and how bulky or tall, or ferny or spiky, things are. I give you some of the combinations that have pleased me. I recount many of the experiences I remember having had with these plants, good and bad, in an attempt to give you a feel for growing them. My aim is to encourage you to try more plants than you ever have, give them a better home, and then dare to do some experimenting on your own.

Some of the Tallest

Many very tall, attractive plants do well in light to medium shade. Cimicifuga is one of these. It is an adaptable plant, but likes best to be in an understory situation. At the edge of a woods, *Cimicifuga racemosa*, often called bugbane or fairy candles, sends up six-foot stems of branched white candelabra from thick, astilbe-like foliage in July. It invariably leans into the light and may need staking, which I do inconspicuously with branches cut from a tree; nothing is uglier to me than a rigid, corseted plant. This plant is a spreader, not invasive, forming good clumps over the years. It needs about a half-day of sun to stand straight, especially after the bloom turns to seed, when the heavy antlers of

Cimicifuga simplex 'The Pearl' is shorter than its cousins and has finer, lighter wands of bloom, so it stands straight. It is also much later in bloom, often barely opening before frost, and holding its pearl-shaped buds for many days as the blossoms slowly open. It is lightly but sweetly fragrant, and has the astilbe-like foliage that makes the family so attractive. This plant is also extremely easy to divide in spring. Just dig it up, divide in four, and put the pieces where the shady garden needs white banners late in the season.

Staghorn sumac grows here in more shade than it would like, and leans out into the sun, coloring beautifully and making a fine background for the border.

green seed pods weigh the tall stems down horizontally over my paths, unless I have propped them.

In my garden, the most utterly spectacular fall presence is *C. ramosa* 'Atropurpurea', which throws dark, seven-foot stalks of beady, purplish buds above its purple-tinged foliage in September, which proceed to burst into long, arching, fragrant garlands of fuzzy white bloom. This is a strong, very tall plant that leans only a little bit, and then only when heavy with seed. Varieties with very dark purple leaves, 'Hillside Black Beauty' and 'Brunette', are available as well, in about the same size and habit, but with black-purple leaves and stems. I have them started among my most golden-leaved hostas at the back of the lot.

A three-foot variety, *C. simplex* 'The Pearl' throws snow-white, upright branched spikes in profusion in late October on a three-foot bush. It stands up nice and straight and is a bright accent that "reads" across a long distance in the shady garden, lasting until hard frost. This plant does equally well in high shade or half-sun, and prospers and divides very well.

The Delicate-Looking Thalictrums

One of the taller meadow rues, *Thalictrum rochebruni-anum*, lavender mist, forms a good stand of aquilegia-like leaves, about three feet tall and as wide, and sends up astonishing seven-foot bracts of small, quivering pink bells with yellow anthers, even in half-shade. I believe it would enjoy

almost full sun if well watered. There are several slightly smaller thalictrum varieties with white, pink, or yellow blooms for delicate tall accents. I like them and try to have every variety I see. I especially like *T. delavayi*, as it has incredibly fine puffs of pale pink, at about my chin level, where I can watch the butterflies work. *T. flavum var.* 'Glaucum' is a tall plant with glaucous, aquilegia-like leaves and pale yellow blossoms. *T. dipterocarpum album* is a mid-sized plant with *T. rochebrunianum's* bell-shaped blossoms, but in pure white.

I also love to have the wild meadow rue *T. aquilegifolium*, which was on my property when we arrived, spread itself gently in my shady gardens. The bluish, aquilegia-like foliage grows to about two feet, and when the blossoms come I have to look closely, as they are subtle: just a short, trembling fringe of yellow-green. The foliage stays nice all summer and accents simply everything to perfection. None of the taller thalictrums take up much room at the base, and all create a delicate effect between ferns and hostas. Several smaller thalictrums are described later.

A Giant Beauty

A massive plant choice for part shade, and one of my favorites, is *Aruncus dioicus*, or goat's beard, which again is most like a huge, shrubby astilbe, some four or five feet high and as wide, with its long, open, snow-white, branched plumes held six feet in the air, not usually leaning over until the bloom is almost brown, when it can be cut back if it looks messy. The plant does best with lots of water, but in my deep, humusy soil it has never failed. It receives less than a half-day of sun and thrives at the east edge of a woodland border. It is so big that it almost seems impossible for the stems to all die back to the ground every fall and be easily removed—but sure enough, that's what happens. It never

needs protection in winter.

A. kneiffii is a three-foot variety, with all its parts that much smaller and more delicate. It likes the same conditions as its bigger cousin but fits into more kinds of plantings gracefully.

Aruncus, like thalictrum, has a miniature cousin that must be seen to be believed. More about that later.

The Tallest Thing in the Border

Macleaya cordata, the plume poppy, grows in either sun or considerable shade, and while it stolonizes and multiplies rapidly, it is well worth growing, especially if it can be viewed with backlighting, when the leaves are translucent,

Left: The tall *Macleaya cordata*, 'plume poppy' and *Lobelia cardinalis* consort well together. The eight-foot plumed stalks of macleaya have large, nicely shaped leaves, which form a background as dense as any tall shrub and show a warm pink infusion of color when backlit by the sun. Tall and bulky as they are, the stalks are easy to pull off in fall and always go on the loose compost pile.

The lobelia forms good seed pods, which I leave all winter for the birds.

Opposite: *Aruncus dioicus*, or goat's beard, is a stunningly tall accent in the shady border, punctuating the dark wood's edge with seven-foot plumes of infinite delicacy and grace. I like aruncus near the front of the border, with low-growing white accents at its feet, close enough so that the plumes are at eye level. Yet I recommend using this shrublike presence to back up substantial plantings of hosta and fern in other areas; it is always lovely in leaf, and it is incomparable in blossom. It is almost surprising to see, every fall, that this enormous shrub is entirely deciduous. This must certainly be a survival mechanism: all plant parts are safely underground for our cold winters.

showing a soft pink through their velvety green. It will top seven or even eight feet, stay mostly erect, and have enormous scalloped leaves and two- to three-foot plumes of tiny, creamy pink blossoms. This giant plant seems to do very well without added water all summer, though it could remain shorter if rain is scarce. I like it rather in the foreground in spite of its density, especially where it partially obscures a vista and creates garden mystery. It is, however, a wonderful plant for the back of a sunny border, especially at a tall fence or a wall. Every year I give away some rhizomatous babies to keep this eager plant in bounds and out of my paths, but I have recently learned that snapping off unwanted stems when they first start up prevents their development and keeps the roots in bounds.

A Toxic Beauty

Some of the aconitum (monkshood) approach six feet in height and do well in sun or shade. While they need support in shade, they are very satisfactory. They provide glossy dark green foliage all summer and glorious blooms with plump helmets clustered thickly down long stems from June until late in the season, mostly in shades of blue, but also in pinks or white. This is a poisonous plant, and I handle its roots and stems with gloves, but I would not like to garden without it. The flowers do not fail until hard frost. Strangely, although the species is said to not like being disturbed, I have had good luck moving clumps of it to different places in the garden. It seems to do best in part shade, and it does like to be kept moist and have the very best humusy soil. The mother clump always remains the most vital, but this is probably because it is in a favored location: deep, mulchy soil in a raised garden, in the north shade of the house but under open sky.

To get more extended bloom, one can find many varieties. *Aconitum septentrionale* 'Ivorine', a lovely creamy white variety, grows only two and a half feet tall and is the earliest to bloom, peaking in mid-June. *A. napellus* is blue; and *A. n.* x 'Bicolor' is white with a blue edge, both coming along in August; while *A. n.* 'Carneum' is a July bloomer, with pale rose-flushed blossoms. My deep blue one is *A. carmichaeli*, which finishes the season in September and October.

Leaf Interest

Ligularia stenocephala 'The Rocket' produces three- to four-foot tapering spires of fine yellow blooms above large, triangular, tooth-notched leaves in sun or shade, given lots and lots of humus and water. It handles creek bottoms and pond edges, but will do just fine in a somewhat drier garden situation with enough shade and water to keep it from wilting. It is dazzling in bloom, especially near the golden-variegated hosta cultivars, and its large leaves are great all season. *L. przewalskii* is quite similar in bloom habit, but with palmately cut leaves. I have both, and they are planted together near a yellow-green interrupted fern and above a royal fern and a planting of trollius. While catalogs say these like shade, in my garden they want quite a bit of sun, at least a few hours a day, in order to bloom. And they are simply gorgeous when backlit!

I like ligularia leaves so much that this year I set out both *L. dentata* 'Desdemona' and 'Othello' at the back of the pond, behind the little clematis on the rocks. They are mysteriously tropical in both size and color: a deep wine color comes through the green of the great, notched leaves. I sometimes cut back the flowers rather early, as they are yellow-orange daisies, not my favorite type.

Cotton Candy Blooms on High

Meadowsweets do very well in part shade and handle midsummer drought quite well. I have one very tall variety,

Filipendula rubra 'Venusta', or queen-of-the-prairie, which I like in my part-sun gardens, though it spreads, and flops to a certain extent after blooming. I use it only in the center of an awkwardly large garden spot right at the foot of our driveway. There it forms a central focus, blooming in mid-summer with pink cotton-candy fluff six or seven feet in the air, and I can cut it off when it begins to lie down. It is very large, probably too coarse for the ordinary garden, but butterflies love it. In my garden it accents the color tone of mostly rose, red, and pink things, along with yellow and pink daylilies. The height is necessary there in the middle of that large triangular garden spot. In its original setting I grew it facing south, but under the shade and in the drying influence of a locust tree's roots. It never grew over three feet tall there, but it did bloom reliably even if I forgot to water it. It is a good old, tough prairie plant, with deep roots.

Even this big plant has small relatives that grace the more refined areas of the garden, as we will see.

Quietly Spectacular

Kirengeshoma palmata is a shade plant that is growing in popularity around here. Unfortunately, it has no popular name. I have a nice mature specimen over five feet tall and as wide. The leaves are beautiful, like sycamore or maple, carried in opposite pairs, and the enormous quantities of strange buds and flowers are points of interest late in the season. It doesn't bloom until almost September. When the buds come they are of all sizes, from small marbles down to peas, and as some grow fatter, a star appears to be painted on their ends. One by one, when it is time, these buds nod downward and open along the marks of the stars, producing two-inch butter-yellow shuttlecocks of blooms which open only a bit at their tips. There are so many of these buds and blossoms that they weigh the sturdy stems down into a

Top: *Kirengeshoma palmata*, while it has no common name, is a plant you will not forget once you have seen it in bloom. After some six or seven years, this one has reached a height of close to five feet and spreads even wider when in bloom. It has good rigid stems, and the only problem you will have with its spread is having to dig up and move plants from all around it so they won't be smothered.

This is not a showy plant, for all its size, but one that invites contemplation. First come the big, sycamore-like leaves on straight, thick stems, then late in summer the interesting round buds and partially-opened hanging flowers.

Bottom: This is as open as kirengeshoma flowers get. It is an understated and tasteful display, long-lasting but quiet.

Right: Hosta fortunei 'Albo-picta' is among the most deliciously colored of the variegated kinds in spring, though it gradually changes to a plain, glossy green for the summer. It is a large, fast-growing plant that can be divided frequently, making a lovely companion for spring bulbs during the time it wears its Joseph's coat.

Ostrich ferns make a wonderful backing for any colored hostas.

Opposite: If one had to choose only one hosta to stand for them all, one could do worse than *Hosta montana* 'Aureo-marginata'. This is a bold plant, sturdy and tough, with long, elegantly shaped leaves. The "painted" brush strokes extend in nicely feathered lines to the very leaf tips, leaving a broad, brilliant cream border. This photograph is a spring view, as later both pedicels and leaves elongate and spread wide, though still keeping a good loft, so that the mature plant is not flat but fountainlike in form.

It is the joy of finding such hostas and their companions that makes us enthusiasts, as we learn to put together differently colored and shaped plants that enhance one another and give focus to the entire garden.

widespread bush, and when the plant is really mature it can take up a lot of space. Be prepared to move plants from around this big husky thing, giving it plenty of room. Nothing, for instance, should be behind it except a tree. Once you get this totally undemanding plant through its first year, kirengeshoma seems to have no natural enemies except aphids, which in bad years can weaken the plant dangerously unless treated. Once only in the years I have had this plant have I used a systemic chemical to rid it of aphids. It has come gratefully and quickly to maturity since that time. Nothing blemishes the fine, large leaves until they blacken and fall after frost. Then I cut off the old stems at the base and lightly cover the roots with chopped leaves.

Hostas First

Hosta is always the first thought in my mind when I think of shade gardening. At the risk of seeming to impose my own taste upon yours, I have to say that I do not think a truly lovely shade planting can be made without at least a few hostas. Learn about them, anyhow. Then you can make up your own mind. If you join your local hosta society, you will hear a lot about general shade gardening at the meetings; hosta growers are voracious collectors of things that "go with" their pet hostas. But mainly you will see the hosta in a new light and will probably be hooked.

Changing Your Point of View

Yes, I am aware that the first thing many new shade gardeners must vanquish is a loathing of hostas! From having grown up with rows of them full of slug holes, clinging dully to life at the edges of driveways or waving weak lavender flower stems above lax brown-edged foliage in bone-dry corners, we have had a poor introduction to a lush and exciting genus of plants. The easiest way to see the best of this genus is to wipe that memory out (and dig it out, if you still have hostas in situations like that!). Pretend you are looking at a whole new kind of plant—which, in view of the thousands of new cultivars, you practically are. I would beg you not to throw these old plants away. Even the commonest of them makes a shining, bright spot in rich soil in deep to part

Top: Nothing in the early spring garden is more necessary to me than the fresh colors and textures of small hostas, spacing out the more fussy spring flowers. Here, *Hosta* 'Chinese Sunrise' proves that it is the main ingredient in this bed, providing a cool background for *Primula acaulis*, shooting stars, and forget-me-nots.

'Chinese Sunrise' is golden in spring and becomes a solid light green later in the summer. It is a prolific bloomer, sending up a thicket of lavender buds in late spring, which add to the mix in a different way.

Bottom: One section of the pondside garden features the bright little *Hosta* 'Kabitan' as an edger. This small hosta is pure gold, set off by narrow green borders on its wavy edges. I keep it divided to accentuate its starry form, using the divisions to extend the beds further. The gold accents of 'Kabitan' are picked up by the foliage of *Iris pseudacorus variegata* in the background and by several larger hostas. The star shapes of 'Kabitan' are low and small enough to set off the pale pink floating bloom of the delicate *Epimedium youngianum* 'Roseum', yet bold enough to enhance the larger plants in the composition.

shade. You might have a difficult shady bank that would look glorious with a solid planting of them, or you might use them as background for other more delicate plants.

If you have even one big, ugly, dull hosta that has lived out its life in the wrong environment, dig it out, tip it up, and saw the root ball into twelve divisions (I use an old serrated bread knife), preferably before growth starts in the spring, but actually at any time. If it's late in the season, cut the leaves off first before digging. You can't hurt the plant. And please—use these divisions as background for newer varieties, as borders, or as specimens, or give them to someone who will.

Obviously, carry out this exercise after having prepared a bed of good soil into which to move the divided plants. However, if you have to move some hostas out of a sunny bed because your priority is to prepare the bed for something else, do make a place for the entire hosta plant (or plants) in the shade somewhere, adding manure and bonemeal to a nice, big planting hole(s), water in well, and wait until next year or until you know where you really want hostas to grow. Divide them at that time.

Uses and Care of Hostas

I am tempted to talk about just my own favorite varieties of hostas, but it would be wasteful to take up that much space in this book; I love so many of them. However, you really must look into these plants if you want to have the most beautiful, carefree kind of garden in the shade. No weeds grow under hostas. Bulbs flourish in their shelter. They nestle with ferns and other fine-textured or spiky-leaved plants to create lush background plantings. There are varieties six feet in diameter and more when mature, varieties that make petite and lively small borders, and varieties that fit in the palm of your hand for the miniature rock gardener.

Hostas come in many leaf shapes and colors, enough to please the most picky perfectionist. The flowers on some are really stunning. There are varieties that bloom early, mid, and late season. Some are so fragrant you will think gardenias are blooming somewhere nearby. Some, mostly those with yellow coloring, like a bit more sun, up to eighty percent, but all will burn in hot dry situations, and all appreciate at least afternoon shade.

A specimen hosta makes a good centerpiece for an island garden along with taller things such as fern, cimicifuga, and thalictrum, and small hostas set off the foliage and flowers of any dainty shade plant you can think of. As for ease of care, I have never heard of anyone actually killing a hosta with bad conditions, though certainly they can be stunted, burned, or crippled in hot dry situations. Lots of water, a manured bed, and good soil will give you a show that will make a believer of you.

Try Daylilies in the Shade

Daylilies are another highly popular, easy, and common species that should not be neglected on that account. When I was a child, I was entranced by my grandmother's clump of lemon lilies, probably *Hemerocallis lilioasphodelus*. These slender little yellow flowers are intensely fragrant, and the plant is a parent of many fragrant hybrids. I brought a portion of her clump to my first home when I married, and it is still with me. Ever since, I have been greedily collecting hybrid hemerocallis. I like them as much for their staunch dependability as for their beauty.

True Survivors

Nothing much really discourages daylilies; not pests, not poor soil, neither drought nor flood nor indifferent management, though of course they do much better with

Top: This corner of the back garden is an ongoing experiment with variegated hosta varieties. In this bed I have been arranging and rearranging colored hostas for several years, changing their positions as they grew and matured. At left front, *Hosta tokudama* 'Flavocircinalis' shows its crisp, cupped form and good coloration, with cream on blue-green, all the better for the brighter shades of *H.* 'Great Expectations' and the plain, dark green *H. tokudama* behind it. *H.* 'Gold Standard' is the most obvious background plant because I use it in numbers. Other gold accents are seen in *H.* 'Sunpower', *H.* 'Moonglow', and *H.* 'Zounds'.

Bottom: *Hosta sieboldiana* 'Elegance' in spring shows its promise, but gracefully restrains its growth while the single, red *Paeonia smoutheii*, which we have nicknamed Memorial Day peonies, come into their own. 'Elegance' is a form with such substantial leaf tissue that it never has slug damage, in my garden at least. Its blue color and large, cupped leaves have made it a favorite everywhere.

good conditions. And they do have the prettiest blossoms. You will find every color from near-white through the yellow-orange-pink-red-maroon spectrum, from huge, eight-inch blooms all the way down to tiny two-inchers, with clean, pest-free, gracefully pointed foliage. They love sun, but I beg you not to forget them in your partly shaded gardens. They are quite willing to star in different circumstances. Blossoms will be fewer without full sun, but will stay more colorful, and some varieties will glow like lamps in your mostly green shade gardens. Ferns, hostas, and especially astilbes are glorious with certain harmonious daylily colors. Growing them in shade may take some experimentation. There are cultivars of hemerocallis that will pout and decline with a few hours of shade, but you can find others that remain vigorous and put up quite a lot of bloom. When, toward fall, any of the leaves become ungraceful, they are easily pulled up. Like hostas, daylilies come in many sizes and types, and all grow into nice clumps in a year or so. None is invasive except the old ditch-lily orange ones, which you should avoid. All that daylilies ask is enough light, water at blooming time, and division about every three or four years. They give a great deal for such a small investment.

Something a Bit Exotic

Tricyrtises are odd, attractive plants that have been popular with Japanese gardeners for a long time, we are told, but only now are becoming available in this country. Their greatest value to us is that they bloom in late summer to fall, when we really need bold features in the northern garden. They are attractive accents all year, however, making stunning arched displays of long, pointed leaves laddered along the stems when not in bloom. In blossom they are rich and lively accents for the fall garden.

Under the common name toad lily, *Tricyrtis hirta* was

the first I ever saw offered, and it has several cultivars. The blooms of *T. h.* 'Miyazaki' are orchidlike, white with lavender-purple freckles and perfectly beautiful radiating pistils and stamen. The plant is easy to grow and heavily loaded with bloom. *T. h.* 'Variegata' is smaller and the leaves are delicately silver-cream edged, while the blooms are similar.

Another lovely cultivar, *T. macropoda (dilatata)*, grows in an attractive tall vertical with alternate clasping leaves, and the buds form at the leaf axils on the top third (or more) of

Left: Hemerocallis needs no better advocate than 'Painted Lady', as she looks late in her prime about the end of June. This tetraploid hybrid displays the best qualities of the genus: fat, plentiful buds, many scapes, sturdy stems, healthy leaves, and large, richly colorful blooms. Who needs to know that every part of this plant is edible?

Opposite: This is a section of the long border of *Hosta* 'Gold Drop', which holds twenty-four plants created from three dense little specimens given by a friend. This is a good multiplier! And what an easy way to define a long bed of mixed hostas, ferns, and trees. Not every bed should be so evenly defined, I think, but one uninterrupted border such as this gives definition to the entire garden complex.

H. 'Sum and Substance' unfolds its giant pale leaves in the background, with a young *H.* 'Great Expectations' highlighting the foreground. At right center is the already changing *H. fortunei* 'Albopicta', turning from cream to chartreuse at leaf centers. At lower right, *H.* 'Zounds' has not yet achieved the golden coloration of midsummer. Epimediums fill the open spaces.

Top: *Tricyrtis hirta* 'Variegata' is one of the low-arching, smaller varieties, showing its freckled "toad lily" blossoms thickly clustered on top of the leaf axils. The leaves are a soft green, with only a bright hairline of cream at the edges. Like most of its sisters and cousins, this one keeps opening more and more flowers until frost. I find this plant an excellent one to set along the back of the berm on the north side, where it shows over the crest and brightens the landscape nicely until frost.

Bottom: This is a November photograph of a most interesting plant in a friend's garden. My own offset was not ready for a portrait. *Tricyrtis macrantha macranthopsis* is an unwieldy name for such a graceful thing. If I were to be asked to give it a common name, it might be falling bells, as this beauty is known to hang down five to seven feet from the cliffs beside waterfalls in its native Asian environment. Like their cousins, they bloom late and hold their beauty until frost.

PHOTOGRAPHY BY FRANK GREER

each stem. Its purple-freckled white blooms come in September and leave seed capsules, slim and erect, for winter accent. It has reached four feet in good years for me.

A friend recently gave me a very early blooming variety, *T. flava*, which produces freckled yellow flowers, larger than those of *T. hirta*, in June (all the others I have are fall blooming). These are clustered at the top fifth or so of the leafy stems, and they are charming when the ferns are at their best.

Each new acquisition makes me more eager to catch another variety! I recently purchased a very beautiful midsized cultivar, *T.* 'Togen', which blossoms in September and keeps a show of clear white blossoms with lavender edges for many weeks. This is one that grows in a distinct curve; I grow it on a raised bed so it can arch prettily among the foliage of Japanese painted ferns, daylilies, and meadow rue. Then I put in *T. hirta* 'Variegata', which has delicately silver-edged leaves on fairly short stems, and thickly freckled, closely placed blossoms. This one is a very late bloomer, and it leaves heavy branches still full of bloom when the frosts come. Next year I will cut the branches just before frost and have them for indoor bouquets!

A somewhat smaller variety, *T. formosana* 'Golden Gleam', has golden leaves with dark green splotches, and is simply covered with masses of deep purple-speckled white flowers in September. It is beautiful among small golden hosta cultivars.

But the most wonderful and strangest of all those I have seen is *T. macrantha macranthopsis*, which is extremely pendant, needing a wall to allow it to really cascade. In nature it hangs seven feet down cliff walls. Its blossom is different from the others, being long and tubular and a rich, clear yellow, with the mouth darkly freckled inside like a foxglove, and four little bulbous spurs at the base. This plant bloomed the first year I had it, with many buds and blossoms at once, and did not quit until almost frost.

My most recent addition is *T. latifolius* 'White Towers', a low-arching cultivar thickly studded at every leaf junction with large, snow-white blossoms in September.

I have needed no heroic measures to keep these stunning plants happy. The usual minimal fertilization and plentiful application of bark, manure, and compost makes for healthy tricyrtises. You will find a hundred places where their architecture is the perfect accent.

Intermediate Fillers

Astrantias are also happy in shade to part sun, requiring only enough organic material to make a good show. The old name for these plants is masterwort. They are modest but quite lovely, about two feet tall, sending up wiry stems of many small puffy blooms above attractive foliage all summer long. The commonest of them is a greeny whitish-pink, which blends with all foliage and flower colors and lightens the mix. Others come in white, soft pinks, or shades of rose, with *Astrantia carniolica* 'Rubra' the deepest, with a silvery-green puff at the center beneath its fascinating hundreds of stamens. The flowers are quite everlasting if cut when in full color, and astrantia leaves are as good-looking as astilbes out of bloom.

A good solid clump-former, with willowy-leaved thirty-inch stems and soft steel-blue flower clusters, is *Amsonia tabernaemontana*. It likes light shade, and will take a few hours of direct sun. In early summer the flowers light up green leafy shade with their clear, unobtrusive pale stars, then in the fall its willowy leaves turn bright yellow. Another variety, *A. hubrechtii*, has the same blue stars but on stems full of much finer leaves, which turn deliciously peach-to-gold in the fall.

A recent introduction to my garden is *Begonia grandis* 'Evansiana', a cold-hardy version of the "blooming fool"

begonia our great-grandmothers grew as a houseplant. In August it fills the shady garden with drifts of shaded pink and rose purses on two-foot plants with a wide spread of speckled, triangular leaves. It seeds true, so you may have as much of it as you want.

Shining Leaves

The hellebores provide some of the most wonderful blooms of spring, but their leaves are their most important aspect to me. I appreciate the glossy, dark mass of foliage at the edges of my shady borders all summer long, and sometimes through the winters.

Though usually listed for Zone 6 and up in most catalogs, several cultivars of the hellebore have settled nicely into my garden in protected areas. They like a mulchy, manured

At one end of the shady berm I am experimenting with *Begonia grandis* 'Evansiana', a cold-hardy form of an old favorite houseplant. This is so like the houseplant, in fact, that I find its ability to survive our winters hard to believe, but it can—with loads of chopped leaf mulch. Its great wings of leaves and little dangling pink pockets are loveliest in August.

The soft, pale background of *Pulmonaria* 'David Ward' and a variegated kerria are in good scale with this somewhat sprawling plant.

Top: To me, *Helleborus orientalis* is loveliest in its white forms. The big nodding blossoms have the typical greenish transluscency, and are well placed at the tips of every stem. The white "petals" are actually bracts, which last sometimes for two months amid the growing, glossy green foliage. They bloomed well before the daffodils in this bed, but they will persist for some time after the daffs have shriveled.

Bottom: *Helleborus foetidus* had been growing rapidly in its mulchy bed near the path, in the north shade of the house, a mound of long-fingered, glossy leaves. Then suddenly one fall, it took on its mature form, stretching to over two feet in height and sending up its pale green bracts above the foliage, ready to open their bells in early spring.

Opposite: *Hellelborus orientalis* blooms mostly in shades of greenish-maroon, but it is also found in pink or white. It's a plant that loves moisture and humus, and although it languished for a few years in my garden, I have recently made it happy and healthy by setting it in good compost to begin with, and pouring on a weak solution of Epsom salts once a year.

bed, at least part shade, plenty of water, and a dressing in June of a half-cup of Epsom salts in a gallon of water, which really promotes blossoming.

This is a genus beginning to multiply in cultivars, and all make substantial additions to the shade garden with their leaves alone. Their blossoms are like single roses in form, from two to four inches in diameter, and their color ranges from greenish white and snow white through pale to deep pink, purple, or maroon, often freckled, and all are extremely long-lasting in bloom. They love the same conditions as hostas and work very well intermixed with them.

I use them with the smaller hostas so as not to overwhelm the hellebore plants as the hostas leaf out, and have to then move them. I would move the hostas instead. Hellebores do not take kindly to disturbance. Beth Chatto says that if you must move a hellebore, divide it; while blooms are still on it, cut off all the blossoms, dig the entire plant, separate it into small divisions, and replant them immediately. If you move the whole plant at once, she says, you are quite likely to lose it. Heaven knows why the more violent treatment works best!

Helleborus orientalis has so far been the most dependable in my garden, with its many colors, from speckled white to deep purple. *H. niger*, Christmas rose, a snow white variety, is beginning to look more prosperous, but it is undeniably fussier and more tender here.

H. foetidus, a rather tall variety with tall clumps of small, cup-shaped greenish blossoms, is doing exceedingly well along one of the bark paths behind the house, where it sends up its many blossom stems and pale bracts from the center of the plant in the fall, and opens in spring. This variety has slender-fingered palmate leaves of a dark green, very glossy and attractive. I give it a winter wrap of burlap.

I recently ordered *H. hybridus*, a new set of hybrids that

come in dark maroon, white, cream, or pink flowers. I wanted a pink, but unfortunately they cannot be ordered by color. I bought one only, to try hardiness.

If dark flower colors are to your liking, find *H. purpurescens*, which has deep bluish-purple flowers with greenish-purple inside.

Big-Leaved Accents

Rodgersias, with their large wheels of rough-textured green-to-purple leaves, will when they are happy send up heavy, astilbe-like spikes of creamy flowers to accent the heavier hosta silhouettes. They are not generally happy enough to bloom heavily for me, though I have seen them standing thick with blossom stems in English gardens. English gardeners put rodgersia mostly at the edges of water, because their roots like being quite wet all the time. I cannot provide such a location, but I can enrich the soil mix to include more humus to hold moisture. I have just begun to acidify their neighborhood a little. I hope to see both the rodgersias and astilbes respond with lots more blossom from now on. They are so nice together.

I have three varieties, *Rodgersia aesculifolia, R. pinnata* 'Elegans', and *R. p.* 'Superba'.

Astilboides tabularis, once known as *Rodgersia tabularis*, makes huge round leaves, some two feet in circumference when mature, with the stems attached at the centers of the leaves, and send up astilbe-like spikes of bloom (though much thicker and stiffer) in season as well. These are stunning among astilbes, and, like them, appreciate a bit of acidity in the soil. All of these plants, in common with hostas, like plentiful moisture and deep humus. Since I have had very slow development of this plant, last year I applied sulfur here too, and I already had much more bloom this spring. One is never done learning new things!

The Wild Things

It is always wise to use plants native to your area when you can offer an environment similar to what they had in the wild. I try to find plants acclimated to the open woodlands of central Wisconsin and to use them in an understory situation here.

Actaeas fit this description; they grow in many sections of the Midwest, showing themselves as small, cimicifuga-like plants, with triangular arrangements of fernlike leaves rising from the ground with the blossoming stems. They come in various forms, including red, white, or blue-fruited. They blossom in late spring, then set colorful berries in late summer. *Actaea alba,* doll's eyes, produces white berries with black dots on red stems. All varieties are nicknamed "baneberry" because of their toxic qualities. The plants grow two or three feet tall, are pleasant in foliage all summer, have insignificant white blooms, but then charge the fall garden with their clusters of glistening fruit.

In the woods on Washington Island in northern Wisconsin, doll's eyes makes rather small, individual stems, holding its white fruits nicely in the shade of the pines in the excruciatingly thin soil over the Continental Shelf: humusy but not deep. I hope the plenty they find in my garden is not too much for their health. I hasten to add that my plants are not gleaned from the wild. I also wish to stress that the berries of this pretty plant are probably very attractive to children—but they are poisonous. Use discretion in planting baneberry.

Smilacina is a native plant long saddled with the name "false Solomon's seal." That has always bothered me. It isn't false anything; it is its own beautiful self, with its ladders of alternate leaves and its terminal racemes of white blossom turning to red berries. *Smilacina racemosa* is the larger variety, with a dense plume of white blossoms in spring and a large clump of small, soft red berries in autumn. It grows to about two feet or more. *S. stellata* is smaller, with daintier blossom sprigs that of course bear star-shaped individual flowers. These were both native to my lot and present in numbers before I arrived. One has to overlook their habit of laying down the whole stem when the berries ripen, as it is one of their tricks for reproduction; they cannot be kept aloft in fall without supports, which would look awful. They stolonize quite rapidly, but I simply dig them away from lawn borders and set them over in other gardens. I enjoy them everywhere, though not in my gardens of miniatures, where they would soon swamp the daintier plants completely.

Leaves similar to those of smilacina, but alternating along the stem at wider intervals and with the stem piercing the base of each leaf, mark the *Uvularia grandiflora* (merrybells), which hang long, narrow yellow lily flowers down the stems in spring. They were native to our woods, so I have many fine clumps. The blossoms come when the plant is quite dainty and small, but after blooming the stems and leaves grow, multiply, and make a good feature in the shady border.

The largest of the ladderlike forms in the wild garden can be found in *Polygonatum commutatum*, or great Solomon's seal. I moved three-footers from the woods into my shady borders twenty years ago, and now have six-foot giants, with long greenish bell flowers hanging in groups of three or four under the arched stems and turning to black berries in late summer. Since the soil has grown deeper and more humusy, the roots of these specimens reach amazing proportions, sometimes a foot or more long and as thick as a sweet potato. I remove them only when their strong arches interfere with the form of another plant, such as the Japanese maple. They transplant successfully, and I would not be without their wild addition to the effect of my gardens. I especially like to see them admiring their reflections in my fish pond.

Top: *Uvularia grandiflora*, also known as bellwort and, more aptly, merrybells, blossoms when the plants are only about a foot tall and the leaves are few and folded downward, out of the way. The pointy-petalled bells swing back and forth, attracting the earliest bees. The fading and dropping of the bloom is always hidden by the new growth and posture of the leaves and stems, which set up a thick, healthy clump for summer.

Wood phlox and the new leaves of wood poppy are good underplantings; later the poppy plants will grow tall and full, closing in around the uvularia.

Bottom: *Polygonatum odoratum* 'Variegatum' is a much smaller, finer-leaved plant than *P. commutatum*. The variegation occurs in a fine, silver edge to the leaves. Even in the substantial clumps it can form, this plant is always graceful. Something about its elongated, paired white blossoms hanging under the winglike leaves is entrancing. If it really has a sweet odor, however, I have never been able to detect it.

PHOTOGRAPHY BY TOM COTTINGTON

This thrilling jack-in-the-pulpit is a Japanese cultivar, *Arisaema sikokianum*, which I grew from seed. Its firm, blunt spadix is a glistening white in the white interior, framed by an open, standing canopy of rich red-chocolate color. It has two stems of leaves, one five- and one three-leaved, which rise with the furled bud in June.

topping out at four feet, but it really lights up a shady neighborhood. The leaves of polemonium stay green and feathery all season.

My colonies of native *Arisaema triphyllum*, the familiar jack-in-the-pulpit, make enormous, onion-sized bulbs and put up thick stems and large leaves. The "pulpits" are often six or more inches high, and the bundles of red berries on the stems in fall are just as big. They seed well in certain years, and somehow (ants, or mice?) the seeds get carried all over the garden.

An Exciting Experiment

Arisaemas have many collectible varieties. I purchased seeds of *A. sikokianum*, or Japanese rice cake plant, but while every one of the expensive seeds germinated, I lost the entire first crop when I potted them. The following year I bought five more seeds, all of them germinated, and I took some of the little rooted plant plugs and set them out directly in the mulchy garden behind the screened porch on the north side of the house. Yes! One lived, blossomed the first spring, and increased each year! It is a marvel, with a red-chocolate brown exterior to the "pulpit" and a snowy white, sparkling interior, and fat mushroom-topped spathe. Incredible. So far, in its immature state, it makes slender five-leaved fronds and only one bloom. I do hope it lives long and prospers. I like it so much that I am considering trying some other exotic arisaemas.

Polygonatum odoratum 'Variegatum' is a smaller variety at about two feet, with thin silvery-white edges to the leaves and mildly fragrant pendant blossoms. A small gem, *P. humile*, arches its petite eight-inch ladders over a bed of my smallest hosta, 'Tiny Tears', where small ferns and dicentras back them up. It sends its rhizomes out and out, forming quite a patch in a few years.

Polemonium, or Jacob's ladder, is a very different ladderleaved plant for the shade, with a lacy, ferny effect, and it gives the additional thrill of really nice blooms. This is a native plant that has been extensively hybridized for variety. Although it comes in pale blue, near-white, or pink, it is most gorgeous in the true cobalt blue of *Polemonium caeruleum*. This is one of the taller native varieties, sometimes

An American "Bluebell Woods"

The biggest show here in spring, I have to admit, is from *Mertensia virginica*, Virginia bluebells. From their dark, horizontal rhizomes these send up an amazing big, soft-leaved plant every year, loaded with pink-budded blue flowers. These seed around prodigally, making this plant another of the best for giving away to new shade-gardeners. This is the seedling I most often see in thick patches in my bark paths, where the long stems lean over and drop seeds. The large, soft leaves of mertensia look awful when they age, lying around pathetically, yellow and brown, on limp stalks. The plants do not mind a bit if you pull off those stems or cut them back at this stage. If you accidentally pull up a root, plant it somewhere else. There will be plenty left behind. You may also tuck mertensia foliage under surrounding plants, where it will decompose and add to the soil's fertility, though I would not do this under your hostas if slugs are a problem.

A Preview of Daffodils

Daffodils are so much a part of the spring show that they must be mentioned with the mertensia, even though I discuss bulbs in a later chapter. "Daffs" are naturalized throughout the woodsy beds, in drifts of overlapping types, so that as one kind fades, there is another to follow, and then several more. The whole floor of the woods is variously starred with yellow, white, orange, and pink, to set off the Virginia bluebells at the height of their color.

The Woods Turn Pink

After the Virginia bluebells have finished, *Geranium maculatum*, the wild geranium, blooms throughout the woodlot next door and into my garden borders. I know it spreads, and at times I must thin it out, but really it is a pleasure. Its pink blooms are good-sized and the plants grow over two feet tall, so they look lovely just as the maidenhair ferns are at their best for company and other plants are attaining their full height. If cut back, these plants will rebloom, but there are too many of them, and I never get out there in time.

PHOTOGRAPHY BY TOM COTTINGTON

Wisconsin's more open woodlands grow carpets of *Phlox divaricata*, often this snow-white variety. This clump was grown in a private woodlot and transferred to a friend's garden. The blue one is more plentiful in my own understory, but the white one has a nice start.

Color Carpets

A new and increasingly available group of native spring woodland plants is the *Phlox* family, which has many lovely shade-tolerant varieties in blue, pink, or white. I have crowds of the blue *Phlox divaricata*, wood phlox, which seem to do equally well in sunny and shady situations. Colors include white, blue, and a deep purple, especially *P. d.* 'Echo Texas Purple'. These plants last and last in bloom and spread reliably but without choking out any other plants. They make dependable color underneath blossoming trees or other shrubs. The sight of a carpet of blue wood phlox under a budding red cutleaf Japanese maple is not to be forgotten! *P. stolonifera* is a taller type for woodlands, and is found in blue, white, and pink shades.

Top: The best fern for this clay-soil woodland lot has been the *Adiantum pedantum*, the maidenhair. Native to the area, it feels at home in my garden and thrives as I add wood chip mulch to the paths it borders. All it asks besides is a reasonable amount of water. Maidenhair is wonderful in rain; the heaviest downpour only makes the leaves tremble. Never does wind or rain flatten the clumps. Water can drop straight through the densest stand of fronds, straight to the roots: each frond, sitting perpendicular to its shining black stem like the top of a palm tree, is arranged in clockwise-curved pedicels lined with small, rounded leaflets that tip and turn with every breeze, and which quickly dump every drop of water.

When the fern reaches full size in summer, its tangled tops can be loosened and pulled slightly forward by hand to flow down a slope or over a path.

Bottom: Spring fronds of maidenhair fern rise on their shining dark stems, where every part is miniaturized, the leaves like small emeralds set on dark chains. Pedicels and leaves grow with the spring rains, expanding and enlarging until their umbels interlace to form bushy clumps.

The Ferns

Ferns are not only indispensable to the shady garden, they are a whole study in themselves. My experience with them began, as I said, with the native ones I rescued from destruction: *Adiantum pedatum* (maidenhair fern), *Athyrium filix-femina* (lady fern), and *Matteuccia pennsylvanica* (ostrich fern), all of which were native to the site.

The first ferns I purchased were *Osmunda claytoniana* 'Interrupted Fern' for its chartreuse coloring and upright form, *O. cinnamomea*, cinnamon fern, for its interesting rigid habit, *Polystichum acrostichoides*, the Christmas fern, for its long, narrow evergreen fronds, and of course *Athyrium nipponicum* 'Pictum', the Japanese painted fern. Each is incomparable as an accompaniment to all other plants. I have recently been adding many smaller kinds, too, as I developed beds of specimen plants. Every shade planting in my garden is enhanced by some variety of fern, and I almost think the more the merrier. There is an indescribable sprightliness in the border when ferns are growing well, a lightness of form that makes all other plants show their best characteristics.

Rabbits Eat Ferns!

Last spring I missed some of my recently purchased little ferns, which I had tucked into crevices and below rocks in the shady berm. On looking very closely, I saw bitten-off stems! I could hardly believe that rabbits ate ferns. I quickly went for the blood meal and spread it evenly over that berm. All of a sudden, practically overnight, I had fern babies. Then I began to notice a lot of young *Hosta venusta*, one of my minis, popping up. I had forgotten them, and they and the young ferns had been repeatedly sheared by a family of baby rabbits so they never had a chance to show green. One application of the blood meal did the trick, as I applied it so thickly. Even rain didn't wash it off, and in fact I could smell

it myself a little when it was wet. No wonder the rabbits avoid it. But isn't it worth it! From this day forward, I automatically apply blood meal on that garden as soon as green shoots appear.

The Ephemerals

Many of the best small shade plants are early spring-blooming ephemerals. Most of them disappear, leaves and all, at some time later in the season and come into bloom with the earliest bulbs next spring. *Sanguinaria canadensis* (bloodroot) I have in clumps all over the back garden; if it grows on a hill, above a path, or on a berm, its seeds will wash down and colonize lower spots with a will. I am repeatedly surprised every year when I first see it in full bloom, no matter how closely I think I have watched for its budded stems. It simply pops up overnight, before the leaves are showing, and opens with the first rays of the sun. The white petals actually grow as they stay in bloom over many days, so that the flowers get bigger. By the time the petals drop, the leaves and stems have begun to grow, and this goes on until the leaves are substantial umbrellas, about a foot tall.

A double form, *S. multiplex*, is making itself at home in the front berm, and while I usually prefer single blossoms on wild plants, I must say this little waterlily-thing is a wonder. Its blossoms are thick and domed, with lots of pointed white petals, yet the plant is just as hardy as the single variety, increasing each year. Multiplex is not a hybrid, but a naturally occurring variant.

One ephemeral I am very fond of is *Dodecatheon meadia*, our native shooting star, because when I first moved here I could walk up the wooded hill and see them by the thousands, where it is now all lawns, streets, and houses. I "rescued" enough of these lovely plants to start a good clump. Mine are nearly pure white, so I have purchased *D.*

jeffreyi in order to have deep pink ones. Those in the back, in more shade, seem pinker, but they do not thrive quite as well as those in the front, where the shade is lighter. The punctuation marks of shooting star stems and seed pods below the front berm, along the brick walk, seem to aerate the low groundcover of forget-me-nots, dianthus, and primulas early in the season, and I leave them until they compete with the daylily stems, or fall over. Then I cut the dry pods for winter bouquets and scatter the seeds everywhere I think they will grow.

Hepaticas will bloom here, I'm sure, as they are northern woodland ephemerals—but not for me. It is strange, but some things elude each of us. I hope to find the secret of growing hepaticas some day. One can purchase nursery-propagated *Hepatica acutiloba* or *H. americana*, a round-lobed variety, and both have lovely, cupped, lavender-pink flowers with whitish centers.

Dutchman's breeches, *Dicentra cucullaria*, is all over the place, settling mostly under shrubs, where its white panties hang out with the wood phlox in early May. Squirrel corn, *D. canadensis*, is similar, but has more fernlike foliage and slimmer, pinkish blossoms.

Dentaria laciniata, cut-leaved toothwort, is a welcome light presence on the west bank, near the dark-splotched leaves of the red trillium. It grows about ten inches tall and has nicely lobed leaves and clusters of white flowers.

I have trilliums I purchased and trilliums given to me by friends with big woodlots. They are all mixed up now, so that whether I have one species or another I cannot tell. The clumps are growing larger annually and make a long-lasting picture under the trees and along the paths, drifts of white when they are fresh, palest pink as they age.

The one clump I can always distinguish, in or out of bloom, is *Trillium sessile*, called spotted dog or wakerobin,

Page 91: When a neighboring building or fence calls for some screening and there is room, *Matteuccia pennsylvanica*, ostrich fern, is a most welcome presence. The entire area at the far north end of the yard had been under thick wood chip mulch for several years when the neighbors built this tall fence, so it was fertile ground for the ferns and hostas. When the ferns "walk" out into the hosta plantings, they are cut back and moved to other border backgrounds. In my eyes, the entire planting is much more natural and beautiful with those large ferns along that fence. Children love it, too, because behind the ferns is a "secret" path bordered with wild flowers, the ephemerals of Wisconsin's woodlands.

Opposite: Overhanging ferns and grasses make an ever-changing pattern of shadows on the waterfall. Bloodroot and narcissus precede the ferns, and *Myrrhis odorata*, sweet cicely, soon grows to almost overwhelm them.

PHOTOGRAPHY BY TOM COTTINGTON

Top: *Sanguinaria canadensis*, bloodroot, is a most welcome sight in early spring, increasing its colonies where either wind, runoff, or mice have spread its seed. I find this plant unusual in that growth occurs not only in the size and length of the leaves as the days go by, but also in the flowers, their stems actually growing taller and taller, and the blossoms larger and larger, until the petals fall.

Bottom: The woodsy beds in early spring give only a hint of the towering, heavy growth to come. Pulmonarias have begun to blossom, along with the lamiums and sweet woodruff, the trilliums are still snowy, and the Virginia bluebells are in their final, rather gawky stage of bloom. There is always a thick stand of *Smilacina stellata* ready to leap out into the lawn. Its clusters of small, star-shaped blossoms are held in a plume at the end of the stalk. *Cimicifuga racemosa* has formed a nice colony at the foot of the oak, also; if I did not thin it out I believe it would take over the bed. And way at the back, the white bleeding hearts hang out over the low growth.

In the right background the berm can be seen in the process of revision.

with its spotted leaves and close-clinging, down-facing, stemless maroon flowers. This one seems to thrive in a dry, shady spot with virtually unimproved soil alongside the house. That is a secluded location, and it has such a thick colony of wakerobin that I plan to move out a few divisions. I have other places where it will be more visible.

No amount of fussing has ever enabled me to grow pink lady's slipper, *Cypripedium acaule*. I have tried valiantly to use acid peat and additives, even compost with threads of fungi, to create a good environment for the beautiful pink lady's slipper, but alas, she does not like my neighborhood.

I do have a clump of *C. calceolus*, the yellow lady's slipper, which is throwing a few more blossoms every year. Nothing spectacular, just a slow increase. It may need more isolation than I can give it, and I should perhaps move it to a place where there are fewer competitors; the trouble is, there is no such uncrowded space in my garden.

Pest or Treasure?

I would never be without violets. I have many varieties colonizing freely in the woodsy patches, and I remove them only when they are close enough to the edges to throw their seeds out into the lawn with too great abandon. (I hand-pull unwanted seedlings from my pesticide-free lawn!) I have a snow-white, scentless variety that is so visible across the lawn it looks like a houseplant, and after blooming it makes huge, foot-tall, heart-shaped leaves as attractive as ginger. I have *Viola cucullata* 'Freckles', a variety with blue speckles on white. I have a yellow stemless and a white one, and I have the ordinary blue ones, white ones with purple hearts, and purple ones. In the front berm I have *V. labradorica*, a tiny treasure with small purple leaves and masses of small deep blue blooms in May. Yes, they all seed and spread. I don't mind, since they are shallow-rooted, and where I have them they will not choke out any plant I have. When they get too thick and it's time to cultivate and mulch the beds, we often have a big removal party. My friends with fifty acres of woodland gladly come and pick up bushels of mixed violets, which then go off to a happy new home.

Variety in the Shade

You can get a myriad of other exciting effects in a partly shady situation if you look for spiky plants like Siberian or other shade-tolerant irises, some most exciting in variegated leaf colors, and place them near the feathery-fronded ferns and mounded hostas. The Siberian blossoms are gorgeous in their season, with the new cultivars showing broad, flat faces of rose, pink, white, purple, every shade of blue, and even yellow. They will do better in full sun, sending up more blossoms, but they are quite lovely in half-shade. I have several Siberians, from white through rose to purple, in groups of three clumps of like color, in the garden between the brick walk and the brick garage wall, and a very large *Iris sibirica* 'White Swirl' near the pond in back. A pale blue Siberian, whose name I have lost, sends up its clear accents in several areas, incredibly beautiful with every combination of plants.

I. pallida 'Variegata' is lovely for me, with swordlike fans boldly streaked with cream. Its pale blue blossoms are nice, but I treasure it most for the lasting accent of its striped leaves.

I. pseudacoris, the yellow fleur-de-lis of French history, is tall, stiff, and attractive in any cultivar, but its variegated form, *I. p.* 'Variegata', is a most stunning accent plant because of its three-foot height. These have not bloomed well for me, and it may be that I must move them into considerably more sun. I will nevertheless leave a piece of the variegated clump in the shade garden just for the leaves.

A shade garden without some of the miniature iris gleaming around its edges is lacking in perfection. *I. cristata* is

Top: *Cypripedium calceolus*, yellow lady's slipper, is not a rapid spreader, but I am content merely to have it return every year, early in June, in the humusy bed it favors. Bedstraw forms a sticky but attractive background for its handsome long leaves.

Bottom: An unnamed white violet has come to be as much a part of spring here as the trilliums, and nearly as showy. The blooms are large and pure white, with good petal substance and almost none of the purple center stain of *Viola* 'White Czar'. They are raised well above the leaves at bloom time for a spectacular show. While they do not have fragrance, that most prized of violet characteristics, they are a beautiful white presence in the spring garden. After blooming, their leaves grow to about a foot tall and become very large, spreading their broad heart-shapes into clumps that make good groundcover.

Top: *Iris cristata* is the absolutely perfect woodland border plant. In May, the neatly marked flat blooms stud the plants for a week or two, and the plants increase rapidly. Loving shade and humus, *I. cristata* will surround a rotting stump, a big rock, or a living tree, or give that delicate finish to the edge of a path. All it asks is that you do not expect it to compete with any vigorous groundcover or overbearing plant. It looks good all year, with its paring-knife blades of leaves on their flat hands of rhizomes.

Bottom: *Dictamnus rubra* 'Alba', the white-flowering form of the gas plant, is one of the best of those pure whites for lightly shaded beds. The blossoms are reflexed, with many curved white stamens, and as handsome as any orchid. This is an undemanding plant, tolerant of soils and neglect. It blooms along with the wood phlox, which has spread to provide a cool blue carpet in several shady beds.

the tiniest, with its fans of leaves lying almost flat on the ground, and spreading nicely, with lots of upward-facing, pansy-sized blossoms of white, ice blue, or deep blue on very short stems. It is infinitely divisible and a good friend-making gift, always thriving even better for you after you have given some away. It is the earliest of the minis to bloom for me.

I. pumila I have in that intense red-purple which does not fade into the background but glows richly, setting off the daffodils and the other small early bulbs. It blooms at about four inches, forming good clumps in the borders. I love these small irises in my part-shade gardens, where the German bearded ones do not do well.

Good Blossoms in Shade

While a variety of leaf color and texture is most satisfying, there is no doubt that the occasional blossoming plant is needed in the shade garden. Pale-colored blooms are especially good in shade, I think, especially if some of the foliage in the garden is variegated with white or gold.

I like to plant *Dictamnus albus*, the white gas plant, in a somewhat shady spot, though I believe it will take some sun. It is as clean a white as you can find. It grows up to three feet tall and as wide, making a substantial bush. The blossoms of dictamnus are single and held on upright terminal racemes. Individually the blooms are nearly two inches wide, and their trusses are quite showy. *D.a.* 'Rubra' has mauve-purple blooms traced with dark veins. The leaves of both are glossy and compound and emit a lemony odor when bruised, but be warned: if you are among those who are allergic to the oils in the leaves, touching them will leave you with a sun-sensitive blotch of scaly, itchy rash. I simply take care not to let any part of the plant brush bare skin, and I do not cut the flowers for bouquets.

This plant has an amazing tolerance for dry shade; I had

a pink one for many years, growing in that often-mentioned dry area beneath the neighbor's locust and my maple tree. It had been blooming contentedly there, then failed to come up one spring. Had it had too much of a poor thing? Had a disease gotten it? Or had it merely lived out its life span? I do not know.

You are probably aware that gas plant is supposed to emit a flammable gas that can be lit with a match. It's true, it can be done, but only on a very still, hot day, and you must hold the lighted match slightly below and near the open flowers. If conditions are just right, a thin, clear flame will whoosh up the blossoms for a second, not hurting a thing— unless your hair is hanging too close.

Pale Spikes

Digitalis ambigua, a perennial variety of foxglove, gives a pale yellow accent in late summer, sending up increasingly large colonies of slender bloom spikes in partial shade. The variety *grandiflora* has larger blossoms for a bigger show. This plant works well against the dark wheels of rodgersia and a background of ferns, especially where it picks up the precise tones of *Hosta* 'Gold Standard'. It is amusing to see the stems of this digitalis grow longer and longer toward fall and to watch them undulate out over the beds, bearing just a few yellow blooms at their tips. This seems to be a reproductive technique, as eventually the stems actually touch down, thus giving the dropped seeds a good chance of sprouting.

Having seen the thick, lush columns of the larger and more colorful foxgloves in English gardens, I came home and tried several varieties. I think we are doomed to disappointment in our northern growing zone as far as these flowers are concerned. We just cannot provide the conditions that make them happy. I have not had luck with any other digitalis than *D. ambigua* as a perennial. *D. purpurea*

does set seed for me, however, coming back as a most welcome biennial, with crowds of seedlings that I carefully sort and set out in a sandy bed. I move these to permanent settings the following year.

Columbines for Movement

The sight of long-spurred columbine blossoms dancing on their thin stems always reminds me of visits to Tower Hill State Park in Sauk County, Wisconsin. This is a limestone bluff area of the Wisconsin River, where, among many other wild flowers, the native *Aquilegia canadensis* grows out of the vertical rock faces, hanging its red and yellow blossoms all the way up the rock. In my neighborhood they were called honeysuckles and indeed we used to bite off and savor

Aquilegia alpina is not a tiny plant, as its name suggests, but neither is it ever leggy or tall. It forms a solid clump and puts its blossoms close around itself, enough of them to signal blue all across the lawn and invite closer inspection. The spurs are short and curled inward, and the short cups are snow white, giving this plant the same impact as a delphinium, but closer to the ground.

Astilbes do many things for the garden that no other kind of plant can do. A planting that contains even one astilbe can never be boring. Every variety adds a different kind of light, feathery blossom accent, with pale or rich color, and attractive foliage. The fact that astilbes can do this in either shade or nearly full sun makes them all the more amazing.

Astilbe japonica 'Peach Blossom' is a case in point: its effect here among the hostas, in the right light, is totally enchanting.

the sweet little balls of nectar at the tips of the spurs.

Aquilegias are wonderful plants that take everything from light to almost full shade, though in my garden they thrive best with morning sun. Not long-lived, they are still very much worth growing. They blossom for six to eight weeks, if deadheaded, and come in many forms and colors.

Though most are known for their long spurs, *Aquilegia flabellata* has very short cups and curled spurs, and blossoms so thickly that the color calls far across the lawn. I have a white *A. f.* cultivar and a blue one that has white rims to the cups. *A. vulgaris,* granny's bonnet, has stubby little bright mauve flowers that come so thickly they make the plant look like a solid pink shrub.

Long-spurred *A. chrysantha* 'Silver Queen' has enor-

mous winged blossoms with flared spurs spreading wide open; they are the ballerinas of the garden.

Aquilegias are easy of culture, though not very long-lived. They need careful siting; they are quite watery in structure and susceptible to crown-rot if not set in well-drained soil. They do well on a berm, especially if they have a pocket of good humus. They are subject to a few pests; watch for leaf borers and a very small caterpillar (worm?) that can denude plants in a few days. Last year all my plants were totally denuded by these little creatures. Seedlings popped up in late summer, and came up the next spring, but they were not true to color. Whatever care you take of aquilegias, they are short-lived. Buy new plants annually so you will not be without them.

Astilbes for Color

My most colorful blossoming plants for shade are the astilbes; they come in every size from three inches to five feet tall, in every shade of white through deep red, and in feathery arrangements of fluff that are substantial enough to make a true color statement and which complement every plant, especially those with large leaves. No shade garden is complete without some varieties of astilbe, and they do not balk at sun if they are watered and fed well. I use them in masses, by color.

Choice is quite a personal thing, but *Astilbe taqueti* 'Superba' is a tall, mauve presence that should be planted for a late accent, and *A. arendsii* 'Fanal' is a rich red that keeps some color long after the blooms are over. *A. chinensis* 'Veronica Klose' is a really beautiful thing in bloom, making sturdy clumps about two feet tall, and at least as wide, of a rich mauve rose-purple. The seed heads do not brown, but keep a rosy color into fall. This one divides like a charm, if you have the strength to chop apart its firm roots. *A. japonica* 'Peach Blossom' provides those heavenly pink, airy fronds that make the entire garden come alive.

Old-Fashioned Favorites

Dicentra spectabilis, bleeding heart, is to me a necessary presence in any shady garden. It makes large, glorious plants in early spring, with succulent stems, attractive leaves, and totally spectacular (hence the name!) sprays of large heart-shaped lockets. The familiar pink bleeding heart, *D. s.* 'Rubra' is beautiful, and I would not be without it, but *D. s.* 'Alba' is sheer glory among emerging ferns, daffodils, and fritillarias. Its white is pristine and breathtaking. The word fresh might have been invented just to describe white bleeding hearts in bloom.

Though the long branches and soft leaves of these

Dicentra spectabilis 'Alba', the white bleeding heart, is so pure in its presentation that it creates an almost spiritual effect. Although the old-fashioned pink one is lovely, when alba is in bloom it is impossible to not stop and gaze on her perfection. She is beautifully decorated with the familiar heart-shaped lockets in the whitest of whites, tapering in size to the smallest pinky-nail, all hung out in descending order on clear olive-green ferny foliage.

The leaf miner may disfigure the leaves, but it happens after flowering and is never fatal. There seem to be no other pests that disturb it. As long as *D. spectabilis* has good drainage it will simply grow larger and more spectacular, earning its name year after year

Trilliums add their white triangles to the picture here, lasting even longer than the dicentra.

plants deteriorate to limp yellow ropes in mid to late summer, that is a minor affair. I go to the trouble of bending and folding them under nearby ferns and hostas, or I pull out the most yellowed ones.

The Small and Dainty

Many of the large and midsized perennials used for bulk and color in the middle of the garden have small relatives that can add charm to borders and rock gardens. Some

'Nana' is a perfect small copy of the big queen-of-the-prairie, which produces the same puffs of pink cotton candy at near-er ground level; some years, only about one foot tall. For me, it grows in the sun on the front berm, where it blooms in July and shows off its spreading clump of maplelike, crinkled, soft-colored leaves all season.

The smallest varieties of thalictrum are even more enchanting. I have two, *Thalictrum kiusianum* and *T. kore-anum*. They are similar to one another in leaf and form, with thread-thin pedicels and lopsided disks for leaves. The first is a bit over a foot tall and the second under six inches. Both stay in bloom for three to six weeks in spring, with delight-ful pale puffs like those of *T. delavayi*. Seedlings abound, and I will heartlessly remove commoner small plants from my special gardens to make room for them rather than give them away. Only a real friend and a good gardener gets these seedlings from me, and I treasure the fact that both of mine were given to me by a friend.

Tiny Bleeding Hearts

Dicentras have wonderful small cousins too. The small-er cutleaf Dicentra cultivars, *D. eximea*, in many named vari-eties, are lovely along paths and rocks, and they bloom off and on all summer, with modified lockets of white, pale pink, or rose. They like part shade, but do very well in sun if well watered, and seem to bloom more lavishly with more light. I have used these plants in both shade and sun, and as long as they are provided humus, have a bit of space to themselves, and do not become overwhelmed by larger plants, they bloom all summer. They are, for me, less than a foot tall and very delicate in appearance. They look best if planted among dainty plants, and they really shine in my garden of miniature hostas, accented by a few of the tiniest daylilies and astilbes.

of these I have mentioned in passing, but they need to be discussed in context with other small-scale plants.

A two-foot relative of the tall *Filipendula rubra* (queen-of-the-prairie), *F. purpupea* 'Elegans' is a short variety with more deeply cut leaves and the same pink bloom tufts as queen-of-the-prairie. An even smaller variety, *F. hexapetala* 'Flore plena', is just as dependable, sending out a one-foot tall froth of pure white blossom over a rounded ferny mass of foliage. This variety, I think, likes more sun, but is equal-ly hardy and tough.

I have only recently discovered another: *F. palmata*

Corydalis lutea is said to be such a spreader of seedlings in sun that friends have had to weed it out of cracks in the walk. For me, it has never survived in the conditions near my sunnier front walk. Apparently it relishes the shade and protection of the back berm, where it has its pocket of humus and a place to settle in. If there are seedlings, they will be welcomed and moved all around the back garden, where the continuous yellow bloom will brighten the borders.

Corydalis

Similar in texture and form to the smaller dicentras are the corydalis. I love them, and am especially tempted, year after year, by *Corydalis flexuosa* 'Blue Panda' and 'China Blue'. I have to say that I have not had any success with these dainty blue ones. Perhaps it is the neutral soil; some of the better nurseries specify acid humus for corydalis. Better for me, though, to stick to *C. ochroleuca*, a charming and long-flowering creamy white bloomer, and the more common *C. lutea*,

a yellow bloomer that will seed around in your garden, your brick path, and your lawn if you let it. It is easy to keep in bounds, however, and welcome for its hardiness. (If you are unsure of pronouncing this Latin name, accent the second syllable as a short *i*.)

Small Astilbes and Look-alikes

The small *Astilbe chinensis* 'Pumila' makes a good border plant at under a foot in height. It spreads just enough to make a thick frontal hedge to a perennial bed and to provide plentiful divisions for friends. Its only fault is that the blossoms brown off after blooming, rather than holding color.

My favorite small astilbe is *A. simplicifolia* 'Sprite'. It grows just over a foot high and a bit wider, and has a most decorative way of spreading out and carrying its silvery-pink sprays of blossoms. These do not turn brown or dull after blooming.

Then there are several very small cultivars of astilbe that I like very much in an up-close situation, such as on a low berm or along the edge of a walk. *A. s.* 'Insriach Pink' is one of the nicest. It forms a substantial but delicate clump of fine reddish foliage, with the finest of pinkish-white sprays of blossom at about six inches tall. It is beautiful all season and as hardy as an oak.

Even tinier cultivars, such as *A. s.* 'William Buchanan', look best in the rock garden, nestling into crevices and corners and surrounded by gravel, throwing their snowy white sprays up only five inches or so. These, I find, like more sun than their larger relatives (though not hot afternoon sun), and they survive without as much water and fertilizer.

A plant with a (somewhat) similar texture and appeal to the little astilbes is *Aruncus aethusifolia*. Its foliage is extremely fine, and its small white blossom spikes stand only six to eight inches tall, but it makes highly satisfying low, thick clumps in the garden. I like it with Japanese painted ferns, small thalictrums, fern-leaved dicentras, and miniature hostas. You will hardly believe it could be related to the giants *A. dioicus* and *A. kneiffii*, though its tiny branched white spikes of bloom are precisely theirs in miniature.

Down the Primrose Path

Primulas are famous for earliest bloom, showing an amazing spectrum of color that happens along with daffodils

PHOTOGRAPH BY TOM COTTINGTON

PHOTOGRAPH BY TOM COTTINGTON

Top: *Primula auricula* comes in several shades of clear yellows or reds, from bright to deep, each with a rich golden eye. It grows so well in this area that I divide it almost every spring, even sometimes after it is in bloom. All it needs for encouragement is plenty of compost and maure.

There is something about the cheerful, gaudy faces of this primrose that sets off masses of daffodils and tulips to perfection. I like to use them as borders for the spring gardens.

Bottom: Because of its petite size, only about four inches tall, *Primula* 'Wanda' shows at its best in a raised garden, with rocks to set it off. The blossoms last for at least two weeks, so that, while it appears in a nearly bare garden at first, it soon has the delicate leaves of small rock garden plants for company. Buds keep opening for many days.

Right: *Epimedium alpinum* carries its flowers low, and if you do not clip back the evergreen foliage in April, you may miss them altogether. The leaves will grow back, covering the dropping blossoms and forming a close little roof of triangular "shingles," each leaf edged in a dusting of red. It is a small miracle the way the pedicels angle back and forth so that the new leaves overlap and fill every opening in this miniature "roof."

In spite of their having small blossoms, epimediums arrive in such starry drifts that they create a real presence in the spring garden. Plant some late-blooming tulips to bring out their colors!

Opposite: Winged, spurred, and dancing on hairlike stems, epimedium blossoms are supreme companions for small bulbs and new fern fronds. Their leaves are unique not only lovely in their shapes and tints but also strangely balanced and overlapping on their oddly branched pedicels, forming pleasing arrangements at all times. These plants are among the small treasures of the spring garden, to be savored on those slow, contemplative walks with only birds for company. *Epimedium cantabrigiense* has some of the smallest blooms of those I grow, uniquely colored in orange and yellow.

and small bulbs. They all love shade, at least in the afternoon. *Primula acaulis* absolutely loves sticky clay, as long as it gets plenty of manure and humus, and sets out its posies of bright, round blossoms very early in the spring. This variety is so eager that it must be controlled, or its brilliance will get out of hand. I keep the bright red varieties to an otherwise quiet border, where their exuberance is welcome amidst all the yellow daffodils. In the berm, where many small species daffodils raise their charming small heads, and blue forget-me-nots form a carpet, I keep only the cream and yellow forms of *P. acaulis* so as not to compete. Acaulis need splitting about every third year, in the spring, when their antiseptic-smelling masses of fine, tough, white roots can be forcibly wrenched into ten to fifteen divisions per plant.

P. japonica raises its white-to-pink globes on taller stems and comes along a bit later for me. It is situated in back, near the pond and along the bark paths.

P. denticulata is a shorter-growing form with a globular blossom somewhat similar to japonica, blooming earlier. It is hardy to Zone 3. If you love these early flowers, search for them in seed catalogs because they are quite easy to grow from seed planted outdoors. There are many, many others; I do not raise half the primulas I would like to and have the room for.

An Underused Genus

The many varieties of epimedium are exquisite in both leaf and blossom. These plants should be marked with a big star in the shade garden wish book, as they thrive and bloom even under maple trees in very dry shade. They bloom early, forming clouds of spurred stars, in colors from white through orange, yellow, pink, white, and deep rose, and they develop lovely overlapping roofs of triangular leaves during the summer. I cut back the somewhat-evergreen leaves in March or April so the clouds of dancing blossom will show. Most varieties do not spread prolifically enough to make big masses, and they stay rather low, the largest being only about eighteen inches tall. *Epimedium alpinum* is the most vigorous for me, but catalogs often name as their strongest spreader *E. versicolor* 'Sulphureum', a yellow-blooming variety. This variety is showy in bloom, with the blossoms mostly above the leaves. *E. grandiflorum* has drifts of very large pale pink blooms that stand out clearly in the spring garden. A small white-blooming variety, *E. youngianum* 'Niveum', is perfect on my shady berm, making a ten-inch mound full of white stars. All the epimediums have lovely flights of bloom, but you may never see them unless you cut back the old leaves in March or April.

Top: *Tiarella cordifolia*, foamflower, with its rosy tips, is delightful as a foreground for *Stylophorum diphyllum*, the wood poppy. Tiarellas send up their feathery plumes in late May when hostas and other plants are just beginning to put on some growth. When the large hostas spread their leaves wide later in summer, the tiarellas do not suffer; they snuggle underneath and spend their energy sending out runners and increasing their colonies for the following year.

Bottom: In June, *Lamium* 'White Nancy' turns the white faces of all its leaves to catch the brightest light, then puts out blossoms to match, making it one of the most effective border plants for a dark, shady spot. Behind it, with *Hosta fortunei* 'Aureo-marginata', are the half-grown stalks of giant-leaved *Macleaya cordata*, 'plume poppy', and the short-spurred pink columbine *Aquilegia vulgaris*, granny's bonnet.

Foamflowers

Tiarella is a good plant for dry shade, native to woodlands in many parts of the continent. If given humus and good woodsy soil, it will bear even drought. Most varieties are small, under a foot in height, the clumps having about the same spread. *Tiarella wherryii* has attractive maplelike leaves and a delicate bloom borne in a frothy spike, mostly white but with pinkish tips. This variety forms a groundcover in time, traveling with long stolons. An even better choice for groundcover is *T. cordifolia*, with whiter blossoms.

The newer cultivars of tiarella are bred for leaf forms, with huge rosettes of startling mixed colors from silver to black, or ruby red to pink, which are attractive all season, long after the spring blossom has gone. *T. cordifolia* 'Running Tapestry' has beautifully variegated leaves, and both *T.* 'Pink Bouquet' and 'Inkblot' have pink flowers, the latter with stunning, near-black blotches at the centers of the leaves. I have found tiarellas easy to divide and multiply by lifting and cutting apart the clumps in early spring.

Groundcovers for Shade

Lamiums are bright and agreeable groundcovers in shade, useful for their leaves alone, though they tend to fluctuate from year to year depending upon how they come through the winter. The sharp whites and greens of lamium leaves accent shade plantings to perfection. I like best the very white-leaved varieties: *Lamium* 'Beacon Silver', with its green-edged white leaves and deep pink blooms, and *L.* 'White Nancy', a drift of snow-white leaf and bloom.

L. 'Pink Pewter' has a deeper pink blossom on green leaves with only a central streak of white, whereas *L.* 'Beedham's White' has golden yellow leaves with white variegations and white flowers. This last has not survived for me.

Lamiastrum galeobdolon 'Herman's Pride' is a clump-forming relative, with beautiful pewter-veined leaves and pale yellow pea-flowers, a striking companion for golden hostas. It forms a rounded sphere about a foot in diameter before blooming, and an eighteen-inch mound of the silvery leaves after the bloom fades.

A caution: do not purchase blindly; read the names and descriptions of these plants carefully before ordering. The common *L. g.* 'Avenging Angel' sold by many mail-order nurseries is not a tame, pretty border plant, but a voracious spreader that takes over entire woodlots with its long runners. The named cultivars, on the other hand, are all quite easy to keep in bounds.

The Amazing Pulmonarias

Some of the greatest border and accent plants for shade, in my estimation, are the pulmonarias. There has been a lot of recent activity in hybridizing this genus, resulting in a really gorgeous variety to be found. I use them as groundcovers in some places, as specimens in others. Their blooms are most attractive; they are bluebell-like, and range from pink in bud with blue blossoms, the commonest type, to all-pink or all-white or various shades of blue. The leaves of all varieties form brilliant clumps that make bold statements, expanding steadily into larger clumps all summer long. It is only after the early blooming that pulmonaria leaves come into their own, growing throughout the season and filling the odd shady corner with rich and delightful highlights. Some pulmonarias have leaves nearly completely silvery that reflect all the light there is in dark corners, some are either delicately or brilliantly splotched white-on-green, and some are dark and plain. It is difficult to look at these attractive leaves and remember that they were originally thought to resemble diseased lungs; that's why the plants were called lungwort.

Top: Lamiums are the greatest edge-fillers for shade, with their different leaf variegations and flower colors. This white-blooming variety, whose name I have lost, does not have the showy leaves of *Lamium* 'White Nancy', but it is simply spectacular in bloom. Its quieter leaves, with their slim white center stripe, still make nice edges.

Bottom: Fall does not end the appeal of lamiums. They seem to look their best in the cool, moist air of autumn, with leaves falling around them. Lamiums are often in bloom this late, and their leaves are crisp and colorful, filling in the border thickly under the chance stems of the *tricyrtis*.

Page 108: A bed of ajuga in spring is as pretty as a stand of grape hyacinth and less subject to squirrel and vole damage. Within its shelter, crocus foliage will mature without looking shaggy, and small spring plants like *Iris pumila* will show to good advantage.

The foliage of ajugas is wonderfully varied, coming in shades from deep wine through russets, greens, and grays, to almost white, and in sizes from petite to bold. I use it in various forms at the very edges of borders throughout the garden to bind elements together and finish the hems, so to speak.

Pulmonaria saccharata 'Excalibur' is almost a solid silvery-white with enormous leaves. *P. s.* 'British Sterling' is equally bold, but with a more mottled silver-and-green surface.

P. longifolia 'Bertram Anderson' is one of the best of the slender-leaved, spotted varieties with blue flowers, and *P. l.* 'Pierre's Pure Pink' gives an alternative bloom color on spotted leaves.

One of the most interesting of the many newly named cultivars to come along lately is *P. saccharata* 'David Ward', an all-over greenish white with a jade green border and a deep rose blossom. This variety is extremely sun-sensitive, and it likes best a rather open, light spot of shade with no direct sunlight. It is a jewel when perfectly grown: very large, long leaves in that certain translucent green-white of Chinese imperial jade, edged with darker jade green.

All pulmonarias are readily divisible, and even a very few plants can be developed into a solid bed in a year or two, facing down shrubs or hostas beautifully and giving an especially established look to leggy plantings.

Ajugas

The ground-covering ajugas, or bugleweed, are very prolific in shade, though they will take quite a bit of sun, and since they are now bred in such lovely leaf colors, they can be chosen to set off any planting. Most cling fairly close to the ground, though there are some which form substantial clumps of their crisp, crinkly leaves. They will all creep prettily into paths (and into grass, too, but I give contested areas to the ajuga, preferring to dig my borders out around them and pull out the grass roots). One of my favorites, the tiny, nearly white-leaved *Ajuga reptans* 'Silver Beauty', I use as a border around the shady berm, where most of the other plants are white-variegated. In spring, its blossoms look like a drift of small blue grape hyacinth.

Top: *Pulmonaria saccharata* 'Excalibur' has been the most show-stopping plant in my garden so far. The rather crusty texture of its big leaves seems to gather and intensify light, reflecting it back in the evening in a soft glow. The individual plants are large enough that the uninitiated often take them for hostas.

I have found pulmonarias very undemanding, growing well even when I do not take the time to create a good bed of humus, seeming to make the most out of clay.

Bottom: While their blossoms are really quite beautiful, pulmonarias do not need bloom to be effective in the border. The plants have a habit of filling out gracefully with ever-enlarging leaves when the spring blossoming is over, creating a fresh environment all summer long. There is such variety in leaf shape and color that a collection of different kinds may be used to create lively and interesting border mixes with other plants. This is *Pulmonaria longifolia* 'Sissinghurst White' in May, just before it sends up its snow-white bells.

I like all aspects of *Alchemilla mollis*, lady's mantle, from the pleated new leaves with their finely pinked edges, to the crumbly sprays of chartreuse flowers. But it is the way the leaves hold drops of water that I love best. Anything from a slight dew to a heavy rainfall will leave crystal beads of water high and dry on the leaf cups.

Many of the ajugas are quite large and have leaves of rich color mixtures. The leaves of *A. r.* 'Burgundy Glow', for instance, are variegated with red, green, and white; and *A. r.* 'Bronze Beauty' makes a solid, deep purple-bronze accent. The enormous *A. r.* 'Jungle Beauty' forms eight-inch mounds of purple-tinted leaves, with flower spikes up to fifteen inches tall.

The bronze and chocolate-colored ajugas are handsome with Japanese painted fern springing out from among them, and equally, though differently, attractive with the small, wavy, narrow yellow leaves of *Hosta* 'Kabitan'. This is a rich area for experimentation, with boundless numbers of combinations available.

Ginger

Asarum canadense, our native ginger, is such a reliable thing, and so attractive with its heart-shaped leaves in their dark moss-green velvet, that one hesitates to say the shiny *A. europaeum* is better. I have them both and like them either as groundcover or accent, though I must admit I often put *A. e.* in the more visible places, next to the choicest small plants.

But here, too, we have the choice of some with beauti-

Galium odoratum, sweet woodruff, scents the air with vanilla as it steeps in the May sunlight. When it winters well, as under good, safe snow cover, it balloons out into the bark paths, but it is so beautiful, who could mind? It is like baby's breath in the bouquet of this spring scene: a perfect foil for variegated hostas.

If the odor of woodruff blossoms in the spring sun seems familiar to you, it may be because you have sampled a good European May wine. You can make your own version of May wine if you have enough blossoms next spring. Say you wish to have a party on a Saturday night: cut a good handful of blossom stems (leaves too) on Friday morning. Cut about a two-inch-thick bunch of stems. Put a rubber band around them and tie a long cord to it. Take it into your dining room and hang it from the chandelier over the dining table so it hangs only an inch or two from the table. Let it wilt a few hours. Friday evening, place a large bowl under the wilted bunch, pour in a bottle of Rhine wine to cover the herbs, and let this stand overnight and all day Saturday, until just before your guests arrive. Then squeeze out the herbs and pour in (gently) a well-chilled bottle of champagne. Flowers or fruit slices are traditionally floated on May wine amid the cracked ice.

fully varigated foliage: *A. shuttleworthii* 'Callaway' has silvery splotches, and *A. takaoi* is tri-colored, with silver and plum and green.

Lady's Mantle

Alchemilla mollis, lady's mantle, is an old standby in the shady groundcover department, and there is still nothing to quite take its place. In my experience it is happiest in light shade with some sun, but it does fairly well in quite dense shade. It is a wonderful footing for tall rose shrubs, even nicer if it can spill over a brick walk beside the bushes.

Babies come up everywhere in the cracks, so you will be able to establish new clumps forever. Alchemilla has pinked and deeply pleated leaves that can hold a drop of water like a diamond in their centers, and the blossoms are a froth of chartreuse that goes well with many plants.

A. mollis has large three-inch leaves and makes a sprawling edger that loves to throw its blossoms out into my paths. These are the plants that disguise the unlovely ankles of my shrub roses. They thrive on the peat and manure mulches I put there, and they shade out weeds.

A. m. 'Auslese' is more compact and tidy, and *A. pubescens*

Top: Watching plants emerge and evolve throughout the season is the essence of gardening. When Canadian ginger first begins to unroll the silver undersides of its leaves, it shows the patten of its growth most clearly. Later, its leaves will interlock into a shiny, packed roof of green hearts, in no pattern at all, and its small brown blooms will be hidden at their feet.

Bottom: Japanese spurge is often discounted these days by sophisticated gardeners, simply because it is so easy, and so prolific. Well, sometimes that is just what is needed! It is great to plant something so dependable. I like seeing the whorls of its glossy, notched leaves march over the formerly bare slope on the west side of the house, running down into the woods from the path.

Only the really intense gardener will probably ever discover the sweet scent of these blossoms. Leaning over to remove persistent tree seedlings one morning in early May, I learned a new reason to appreciate this lowly plant.

PHOTOGRAPHY BY TOM COTTINGTON

is an even more compact form, with dark green, ribbed leaves.

A Ground-Covering Herb of the Ancients

Galium odoratum, sweet woodruff, has finely cut wheels of leaves and heads of small, fragrant white blossoms in May, which are stunning spilling into a woodland path. The vanilla-like scent oil of both blossoms and leaves has been used to flavor liqueurs and wines for centuries.

These plants are somewhat sensitive to dry winters without much snow cover, and many years the only ones to survive for me are those under the shrubs. Take a cue from this and give them a light blanket of leaf cover over the winter. You will be rewarded with lovely billows of fragrant, delicate leaves and blossoms in May and a beautiful border all summer.

Two Old-Time Groundcovers

Good old *Pachysandra terminalis*, or Japanese spurge, must be mentioned. It is pretty used in large drifts, with its shiny palmate leaves. Cultivars give you the option of leaf color: *P. t.* 'Green Carpet' is six to eight inches tall, with darker green leaves; 'Silver Edge' has thin white margins; and 'Variegata' has fascinating dense white variegations. Pachysandra is a bit hard to keep neat, but good if it can ramble and get some sunlight through the trees. When it is happy, it makes its white blossoms in spring. Around the feet of shrubs, ferns, or dogwoods, with bulb plants nestled among the shiny leaves, pachysandra is a lovely, glossy ground cover. I have it running down a shady bank where nothing else would grow.

P. procumbens is a very desirable eastern North America native, quite different in leaf but with similar white spikes of bloom and a neater habit, and it may be making its way into catalogs.

PHOTOGRAPH BY TOM COTTINGTON

I put *Vinca minor*, or creeping myrtle, in the same category as the common pachysandra: common, hard to control, but pretty in its way, and with nice blue blossoms or, in the case of *V. m.* 'Miss Jekyll', huge white ones. I have an old bed of the ordinary blue variety under two arborized lilacs, with lots of daffodils that come up into the myrtle, and a border of hostas to hide the fading daffodil leaves. I would never be able to bear looking at that dry spot without the vinca. The glossy groundcover is just right all summer long.

Grasses for Shade

Grasses and sedges add that incomparable, mobile accent to a shady garden, and it is lucky that we have a few shade-tolerant varieties. *Hakonechloa macra* 'Aureola' is a yellow-and-green-striped grass that will make a large waterfall mound in medium shade and form a perfect accent for the chartreuse and yellow-variegated hostas, which like the same rich conditions and plentiful moisture.

A few of the taller grasses will form satisfactory clumps in partial shade, but they are not suited to the deeper shade of woodsy gardens, and they do not thrive in such conditions. I am using only one at this stage: *Miscanthus zebrinus*, or zebra grass, is doing well here along the west and south edges of shaded beds, where the airy variegation and the soft plumes serve to tie the dark and light areas of the garden together.

Many sedges are available these days, and I recommend them highly for bringing a shady border to life. All sedges take sun to partial shade, though they have differing requirements for moisture. I recommend that you search your local nurseries for compatible varieties and try a good selection to see which ones like your conditions. Just as a sample, the following three varieties tolerate moist to wet soil in part shade:

Carex elata 'Aurea', also known as Bowles' golden sedge, is the most familiar; it is riveting when combined with chocolate-leaved heucheras or bronze ajugas, and differently effective near the brighter of the variegated hostas such as *Hosta* 'Great Expectations'.

Carex pendula, or drooping sedge, grows in some shade and forms most attractive sprays, dropping long catkins in late spring to early summer.

C. siderosticta 'Variegata' is a wide-bladed low form with white edges that will slowly spread into good clumps and provide clean, sharp contrast for the smaller plants in shady rock gardens and path borders.

Other shade-tolerant varieties exist, and good catalogs will help you locate them. I intend to expand my library of sedges considerably!

Page 113: Lamium 'Chequers' has masses of deep rose, pea-flower clusters in late April, before any of the other lamiums are in bloom. Its leaves are neatly triangular, and the wide green edges are sometimes tinged with copper. They are accented by a tapered brushstroke of silvery green.

Sometimes I am so pleased with lamiums that I think they might be my favorite groundcover. There seems to be at least one variety in bloom all season, for one thing, and the blooms are pretty, but that is not the reason. It is the soft variegation in the leaves that gives me the most pleasure—there is no planting that is not enhanced by a border of some kind of lamium creeping out from the edges, mingling with sweet woodruff and other groundcovers.

Perennials for Sun

It seems that proper gardeners never sit in their gardens . . .

but for us, the improper people, who plant and drift, who prune and amble,

we fritter away little dollops of time in sitting about our gardens. . . .

Whatever it is, once started a garden holds you in its thrall.

However irksome it becomes at times, who can go outside and kick a lily?

Mirabel Osler, *A Gentle Plea for Chaos*, Simon & Schuster, 1990

LANNING A GARDEN for sun is quite different than for shade. The main difference is the effect that sunlight has on seeds; weed seeds, flower seeds, tree seeds, whatever—all grow faster and thicker in more sun. A sunny garden can become seriously overpopulated almost in its first year, much more so than its shady counterpart, just from accidental seeds. The soil already holds old seeds just waiting to leap to life as soon as it is turned over, and it will receive more and more on the surface each year as your beds mature. My caution is to cover turned soil, very quickly indeed, with whatever comes to hand, and to keep a good two-inch layer of mulch around new and established plants. This will choke out the seeds already under the mulch. Then when you identify a plant that seeds around, learn to deadhead it before the seeds ripen. If it is a low-growing plant, like forget-me-not, take a scissors and give it a haircut before the seeds ripen. And when a plant begins to be too much for your garden plan, for goodness' sake take it out! Put it somewhere else, or dump it on the compost heap, or give it away. If it simply makes too thick a clump but looked fine as a younger, smaller plant, take a small division, replant it, and give the rest away. If it has the wrong color flower, or roots that choke out neighbors—well, you know what to do. Just be tough.

Some Taller Sun Plants

One familiar old giant, the six- to eight-foot *Eupatorium rugosum*, joe-pye weed, is a good background plant for full sun, if you have a prairie-garden situation. Its huge flower heads are to me a slightly muddy rose color, but it is architectural in proportion and as effective as a shrub in its place. It can be seen in its native form anywhere in the upper Midwest, towering along roadsides or where a creek meanders through a marshy place.

A Warning First

Speaking of marshes, I need to give another kind of warning here about *Lythrum salicaria*, that beautiful, tall, pinkish-lavender-spiked plant that turns our local swamps to a rosy glow in summer, but which is strangling so many of our wetlands. I have already warned of its ground-grabbing propensities. The lythrums seed frantically, and each clump sends down its woody roots deep and wide (try to dig one out!), binding the soil and choking out more gentle plants. It is no longer sold by nurseries in the upper Midwest, and we are asked not to include it in our innocent home gardens. Its seeds travel out to the gutters, down through the sewers, into the drains, and so out to our swamps and lakes. You will not like it anyway after the first couple of years, because it will take over your garden, with plants from four to six feet tall and as wide. I had it once, and though it has been gone from the garden for several years, seedlings are still coming up! Last year I found a seedling downhill in the gutter, perhaps a hundred feet from any plant I had ever grown. The seed must have been lying dormant about three years.

A Few Tall Natives

Veronicastrum virginicum, or Culver's root, is a native prairie plant that makes a good background for midsized perennials. Grown in good conditions, it is architectural and sturdy. It stands up to six feet in height, with a tall lilylike stem having wide leaves growing in spaced whorls. The white blossom spikes are like tridents, though usually with more than three upward-reaching tips, very white. Its only fault, in my partial shade, is that it lies down and reaches for the morning sun. I hate to stake anything, so sometimes I have to take some Culver's root out so as not to have it flatten and stifle its neighbors. If I had more open, full sun, I am sure it would stay upright and probably reach its true height more reliably. Culver's root is a vigorous prairie plant, and it spreads. Only a garden with a lot of room at the back should include it, handsome as it is.

Silver- or white-leaved foliage is wonderful in the summer garden. The taller artemisias, while they do need room, provide this excellent effect better than any other species. Choose one or two of the taller ones for your largest border. *Artemisia ludoviciana* is a four-foot variety with pale coloration and interesting texture, and *A. lactiflora*, at about four to five feet, has rather large leaves of nearly milk-white.

Angelica archangelica is only a biennial here in the north, but it is worth mentioning in context with other handsome large border plants because of its stature and its gorgeous purple coloration. It is said to be a reliable seeder, so that even when the parent plant is gone, there is progeny. Its eight-foot stems, leaves, and flat flower heads show purple of different shades, all lovely with the spiky-flowering prairie plants and the tall silver artemisias. Again, this is a huge presence, useful only in a garden that has room for bulk in the background.

The Heavenly Delphinium

Delphiniums are the dream of all cottage gardeners who have sunny areas, and I like them for their tall, brave wands of color, even though they snap off in a second if weighted with a heavy dew, not to mention what happens in wind. The blue ones evoke the most nostalgia for me. For fifteen years, I had a blue clump of one of the huge *Delphinium* 'Roundtable' series return and grace the fence row at the corner of my front garden, which offered part shade. Finally the next-door trees became too much competition, and the clump almost died out. It had been a lot of fuss, as I'd had to tie the plants loosely to the fence and brace the stalks with cut tree branches. Also at first I removed the weaker stems and en-

couraged giant stalks of bloom, even though the least moisture was enough to bring them cracking down. Later, I allowed all the stems to grow, so they would all be smaller and shorter, and these lasted a bit better. I always cut back the spent blossom stems and enjoyed some rebloom, so I miss them doubly now. I think the advice of the small northern Wisconsin nursery where I bought my plants was what helped me to keep them such a long time: wood ashes, applied lightly over the roots in spring and fall. It worked beautifully for my soil type.

A tip for the serious grower of tall delphiniums: A strong, heavily blooming plant will result if the flower stalks are cut back to the ground for the first three years as soon as they begin to grow. This is a real test of purpose, isn't it? Not every gardener can do it.

D. 'Blue Fountains' is a three-footer that I am trying, and 'Dwarf Blue Butterfly' grows from one to two feet tall, with glowing blue flowers. I suppose I have to admit that the smaller ones do not really fill the bill for me. I yearn after the fat wands of juicy blues standing high above the borders. I am working on a good spot for them in the front garden.

Midsized Border Flowers

The taller campanulas, such as *Campanula persicifolia*, hang blue or white bells about two and a half feet in the air, and lend an enchanted atmosphere that I think is matched by no other plant. *C. p.* 'Telham Beauty' has huge clear-blue, open bells. *C. lactiflora* is a heavy bloomer that provides a blue, pink, or white presence in the midsummer garden, nearly three feet tall, if it is happy, and easily as wide. There are dozens of kinds of campanulas, as different from one another as could be imagined, from the tiniest alpines through creeping mats to lovely clump-formers, several of which I will mention later.

Adenopheras look so much like campanulas that one is even named *Adenophera confusa*. They are beautiful enough in bloom, and undemanding enough of conditions, that their rather coarse form is easily forgiven. These plants are drought-, shade-, sun-, and heat-tolerant, a fearsome combination. Nearly ten years ago I set my large *A. confusa* at the rather shady fence line behind daylilies and other plants and under greedy trees, and I rejoice every season in its towers of big, inch-long blue bells. Every year it forms a more substantial clump, and it has long survived numerous other plants tried in this difficult spot. *A. lilifolia* is shorter and finer, with more delicate, narrower blue bells. This is the form that grows along partly shaded banks of roadsides in this part of Wisconsin. While it is lovely there, it does not transplant well from the wild, and it is a more rampant spreader than *A. confusa*. I do not use it.

Perovskia atriplicifolia (Russian sage) would be lovely here as background, too, with its four-foot white stems studded with pale blue flowers. I have tried it for several years, but there is simply not enough sun. It becomes weak and crippled in even partial shade, never growing to its full height and strength. It needs a good prairie situation, and I could envy the gardener who can give it a home. But I am not fond of the scent of this herb. It is pungent to the point of somehow being "off." I understand it is used in Russia to flavor a vodka drink. I don't want to taste one. I would not expect that it is used in roasting meats, as we use common sage, not with that odor!

In another border I have *Malva fastigiata*, that small relative of the hollyhock, about thirty inches tall, which blooms itself silly all summer long in my shaded border under open sky. It would prefer full sun; it leans and flops in this garden, and I have to use "pea sticks" to prop it up and keep it from lying down on the borders. It is, when I suc-ceed, a lovely pink all-summer filler behind the neater border plants, and it faces down the real hollyhocks along the fence. It seeds itself moderately, but it is easy to move the seedlings, if they are in the wrong place, and even easier to find new places for them.

Civilized Thistles

Have you tried growing eryngiums? To some, they are ugly, but I enjoy their spiky form. I have *Eryngium giganteum* backing up *Liatris spicata* 'Kobold' and its almost sky-blue stems and thistly star-shaped bracts, nearly three feet tall (like a plant from Mars, says one friend), are a sight in August. I keep it behind something shorter and sturdier, such as the liatris, as it even then needs propping up, and has terrible knobby knees and ankles—but it is eye-catching in the extreme. It is backed by heavy clumps of a white *Phlox paniculata*, whose name I do not know because my start was a gift from a friend. I love the white behind the purple and blue combination.

Another thistly-leaved plant that gives a unique accent is *Echinops ruthenicus*, or globe thistle. Its firm, softly blue balls of tiny blossom come late in summer on a plant that greatly resembles the common thistles we remember as weeds. This one reproduces heavily, like its relatives, but it does give a cool, architectural background to late-blooming perennials. Keeping it in bounds involves digging up extras in spring or fall. When cut at the height of color and dried, the blooms make long-lasting winter arrangements. For example, I have a celadon-glazed "cricket-cage" vase, one of those hexagonal, pierced Chinese porcelain pieces that we are told served as insect cages. Together with this pale celadon color and the fluffy foliage of *Artemisia schmidtiana* 'Silver Mound', the firm blue shapes of echinops are perfectly stunning, in an understated way.

Good Accent Color

I grow only a few tall garden phlox, and it is mostly because of my preference for planting thickly. Most phlox will turn to white plush with mildew when crowded. When properly planted and tended, phlox are gorgeous in flower, and their leaves can be kept cleaned up, but I am not a fussy enough gardener to enjoy that work. There are mildew-resistant cultivars now, but no one claims to have one that is mildew-proof. For a truly open, sunny prairie site, I'm sure nothing could give more satisfaction than these colorful perennials.

Phlox paniculata 'Bright Eyes', a pale pink phlox with a deep pink eye, blooms thickly in June, looks wonderful with the roses, and if cut back about a third after blooming will rebloom in September. It is not mildewy until rather late in the year, and then not as bad as most. I can keep my unnamed white phlox clean of mildew, too, with a little effort, but my most successful one is an unnamed old rich pink variety, deeper and rosier than the old species mauve color, and quite tall. I have not seen mildew on this plant, and I love the way it enriches the color mix among the daylilies and peony foliage in the late summer garden. I learned years ago that it is wise to nip out all of the weakest stems of a phlox clump at the ground, leaving no more than four, and to strip the bottom third of the stems of leaves at the same time, thus preventing (you wish) the spread of black spot. My plants do look much better when I do this.

Blue, Blue Accents

You will keep hearing from everyone how rare is the truly blue flowering plant in the summer garden. Everyone loves blue in the garden, and I am no exception. When you do find such a plant and it is not a pest, does not look dreadful out of bloom, and blossoms precisely with its prettiest

The platycodon, balloon flower, is that valuable thing, a dependable tall accent of blue for midsummer. The white and the shell pink versions are pretty in themselves, but this blue is necessary in the garden at this time of year. Without that touch here and there even the pastels of daylilies blur into a "blandscape."

companions, say the daylilies and phloxes, mark it well and remember where you planted it. The platycodon (balloon flower) fills all these criteria, and I do have to mark its place; it sprouts very late. I always lay a stone near where it grows and leave it until the plant shoots. Platycodons have white and pale pink cultivars, which I grow, but their colors do not resonate with the current blossoms of other plants as the blue does.

Stars of the Summer Garden

Daylilies are the quintessential sunny garden plants, taking the main focus from early June through August. They are

PHOTOGRAPH BY TOM COTTINGTON

Top: A well-grown clump of the small, reblooming *Hemerocallis* 'Stella d'Oro' shows its clear golden yellow flowers and the many buds for which it is famous. To stay in bloom all season, these daylilies need really full sunlight, and are happiest when divided every other year.

Bottom: *Hemerocallis* 'Bumblebee' is not large, but its deep maroon halo makes it stand out boldly in the garden. The smaller daylilies are good mixers, fitting in well with other plants of modest size. This is a setting of prairie plants: bee balm, purple coneflower, and *Sedum* 'Autumn Joy', all attractive companions to the small daylily, and all tolerant of the same conditions.

PHOTOGRAPH BY TOM COTTINGTON

not, as a rule, plants to enhance others but to be enhanced by them, if you please. They are the queens. Yet hemerocallis gets a lot of bad press, mostly from people who do not really garden. People of a certain age remember them, as they do hostas, as common, ugly things that take over old gardens and ditches with their dull orange flowers. Our grandmothers raised the fragrant little *Hemerocallis lilioasphodelus* or *H. fulva*, simply calling them lemon lilies, and ignored the big old orange ones by the outhouse. The reputation of the latter for invasiveness was fairly gained, so it is important to know that this trait has been bred out of the cultivars. Now of course those old plain orange things, and the little fragrant yellows as well, are among the parents of hundreds of new hybrids in colors never before dreamed of.

Daylilies are not true lilies, as they do not have bulbs but grow from tuberous roots, raising their slender leaves from the ground. Breeders have performed virtual miracles; thousands of cultivars exist these days, some with ten-inch flowers and many with lovely fragrance. They are available in every shade of yellow, orange, pink, rose, and red, and some are almost white. They come in gorgeous ruffled, crimped, spidery, and curled forms. I am insistent on the use of these plants for a well-balanced perennial garden. Daylilies come in enough sizes that they may be slipped in almost anywhere, in sun or part shade. There are no more satisfactory plants for blossom, or easier plants to raise. They are a beginner's dream.

Daylilies, as I said earlier, are what started me gardening; first to find something to bloom with them, then for some things to bloom before and after daylily-time. They are staunch, easy growers, forgiving of ignorance and bad practice, lavish with blossom. They are undemanding in the extreme, requiring only plenty of water when coming into bloom, and division every four or five years.

Reblooming Daylilies

If you wish a small daylily that will rebloom off and on all season, *Hemerocallis* 'Stella d'Oro' and 'Happy Returns' are sure winners in shades of yellow, and only about a foot tall in bloom. Of the two, it is probably easier to grow 'Happy Returns', which seems to need dividing less often to keep its vigor. *H.* 'Siloam June Bug' also gives a repeat performance, with a typical dark eye. *H.* 'Camden Gold Dollar' is another cultivar with reblooming characteristics, which I haven't tried. It is a bit taller, with bloom flushes in July and again in September. Many of the bigger hybrids will put out some repeat bloom, and if you cut off all the flowers of any of them, early on, while there are still many buds, they will bloom again toward the end of the season. I do not need repeat bloomers, since I already have daylily blossoms continuously from May into October.

One look at a daylily catalog and you will be won over. There is a lot to be said for a plant whose individual blossoms last only one day: nothing blemishes the perfection of those blooms in that short time, and there will be another and another and another for many days, often several at one time, on every scape, and possibly more scapes than on any other kind of plant.

The Showy Peony

Peonies, another old-fashioned choice, are wonderful with hemerocallis—large enough to hold their own, and then some, and providing the greatest background leaves to be found. My own personal preference is for the single varieties, as they hold themselves up and stay fresh-looking better than the heavy double ones, without metal hoops set in around them. Last year I counted seventy-five blooms on the big, single *Paeonia* 'Krinkled White', which has gorgeous yellow centers and parchment-white petals, charmingly

An unnamed single Japanese pink peony is a lovely accent for the shaded west border of the front lawn. Small for peonies, these blooms are nevertheless showy and plentiful, calling attention to their combination of pale pink cups and dark shining foliage against the grooved, pale leaves of *Hosta plantaginea*.

Peonies are hungry, and will bloom in part shade only if kept well manured and watered right through bloom time.

wrinkled. I have others of the *P. japonica*, the single forms, in shades of pink to white.

Plentiful in this area is a certain cut-leaved spring-blooming single peony in a rich, pink-red with a yellow burr center, which blooms in May with the tulips. It has much more finely divided foliage than the later cultivars, and grows quite tall, presenting dozens of its bright blooms. It stolonizes just a bit, pushing a baby out far enough that an occasional plant may be taken up without damage to the main body. It never used to show up in garden catalogs, but I am beginning to see it offered. I know it as a pass-along plant from old gardens. It is *P. smoutheii*, an old variety, brought here from Europe. I have an even smaller variety, of a slightly softer color with even more finely divided leaves, but I cannot name it until a good detective job turns up its real title and provenance.

P. tenuifolia, the fern-leaved peony, is a choice little plant that is a bit more demanding than the sturdier forms but still really hardy to Zone 3 if given its preferences, though it is still prohibitively expensive. Perfect drainage and afternoon shade, along with humusy soil, are absolute requirements for this showy plant. It is of surpassing delicacy, at less than a foot tall in my garden, its stems surrounded with needle-narrow, feathery green leaves, with rather small, deep-red single blooms at the tips of the stalks.

I have only one variety of *P. suffruticosa*, the tree peony, and it is spectacular. The blossoms are the size of large cabbages, a rich pink with a paler pink edge to the petals. In color and form it is exactly like the enameled pink peonies that grace eighteenth-century Japanese "famille rose" porcelains. I now have two plants by virtue of the accidental breaking of a brittle root, which I planted separately, when I was moving the plant to a new spot high on a berm. The soil for this berm was mixed and piled on an existing slope, and I used plenty of humus, so that I can water copiously while the plants are in bud without endangering the roots. The smaller piece of root has now produced a blossoming plant, which surprisingly puts up paler pink flowers than its parent, though just as large.

The woody stems of *P. suffruticosa* seem to prevent the floppy habit common in other types, though the heavy blooms open the shrub widely; mine is nearly six feet across in full bloom. And the blooms are simply stunning, calling attention from thirty to forty feet across the lawn. These stems, needless to say, should not be cut back at the end of the season. The rather large leaves will shrivel and snap off the thick, blunt stalks in late fall, leaving knobs and bumps, and the wood must be left for next year's bloom.

All the peonies I grow seem to like shade in the afternoon; they stay fresh and colorful longer than those of plantings in full sun. I should also say that these plants thrive best when not starved. Manure or peat mulches are beneficial, and a light feeding of either 5-10-10 fertilizer or rose food in spring.

Left: *Paeonia smouthii*, a pass-along plant in our neighborhood, probably came to this country with German settlers in the late nineteenth century. Cemeteries in this area often display vases of these early peonies on Memorial Day.

The leaves of this cultivar are most attractive, finely cut and shining green, holding their substance all summer, and turning a deep bronze in fall. The roots spread more loosely than those of other peonies, sending out stolons which produce small plants far enough from the main root mass that they can be lifted readily, which accounts for their spread around here.

Opposite: *Paeonia* 'Krinkled White' will probably always be my favorite. There is just something about the handmade-paper texture of the big white petals, in their single frill, with the rich yellow centers.

Silver Accents

I am fond of silvery-leaved plants, and use many of the smaller artemisias as garden accents. These herbs are scented, some quite strongly, so be certain you like the smell of any cultivar you select for your garden. *Artemisia schmidtiana* 'Silver Mound' is a pet with which I have had varying success, finally determining that it needs benign neglect and a rough, unfertilized dry spot in full sun to look its best. It forms a feathery, foot-high, bluish-silver mound that sets off blue flowers, the blue salvias and veronicas especially, and is really lovely as a foil for pink blooms. When it opens up and flops, I often shear it back to the roots, and am rewarded by a neat little mound of pale silver.

The larger sedums like the same growing conditions as artemesias, and I find cultivars with purple stems especially complementary to 'Silver Mound'. Yet I think the best combination I have discovered with silver foliage is formed by a few good plants of *Heuchera* 'Pewter Veil' in a corner filled with 'Silver Mound'. The purple is there in the heuchera for contrast, along with pewtery-silver veins for awesome harmony.

Artemisia latiloba 'Silver King' is a bit over two feet and a voracious spreader, but I give it room because its true-silver feathery form brings a garden to life from a distance, setting off the deeper greens and all the flower colors.

A. x 'Powis Castle' is a taller, nearly white-leaved thing that I have had to relegate to the hot western edge of the front garden, where it would back up all the plantings with five-foot white bushes in late summer if I did not cut it back in June. I like to keep it at about three feet, and early pruning does that nicely.

I grow several others, and must add that the smell, color, size, and habits of each are a matter of personal preference. All these plants have clean, sharp, distinctive herbal odors, some of which may be unpleasant to you. *A. lactiflora*

'Mugwort' is most pungent, and I do not like it, though I really enjoy most others. I cut many artemisias at peak color and they dry upright in a vase or tucked into wreaths. They are lovely to handle, but I mainly urge you not to forget them for their reliable silver color in sun.

Daisy-Flowered Plants

The *Chrysanthemum* family has been subject lately to a mad upset in taxonomy, giving us (for a while) several new, long names, all ending in "mum", but causing no end of trouble in both shopping for plants and compiling book indexes. In an unprecedented move, the familiar name has recently been restored to the genus, and we can call them all chrysanthemums again.

Our climate is too hard on the double varieties of chrysanthemum, which most of us treat as annuals, filling in with them when perennials fade in late summer. I prefer the single varieties, anyhow, for their more open form, my favorite being *C.* 'Clara Curtis', which has two-inch single flowers of a good pink, with a bright yellow center. This variety grows about two feet tall and blooms just before the tall Belgian and New England asters open. She is lovely at the feet of aconitums, artemisias, or asters, where her longish stems lean over and fill in around the ankles of taller plants. These plants are oak-hardy and need no fussing at any time, though they do need full sun. *C. superbum*, the shasta daisy, is another favorite, providing huge single white flowers familiar to everyone, and they are hardy and dependable here. Chrysanthemums like to be divided, and they look their best the first year after division.

Daisy-shaped flowers are important in a mixed garden, and the echinaceas provide some tough, sturdy plants with good bloom. *Echinacea purpurea*, the purple coneflower, is not to be done without. It populates and enlivens the garden

Opposite: *Paeonia suffruticosa*, the tree peony, in spite of its exotic appearance, is a cold-country plant, used to freezing winters and part shade. This is *P. s.* 'Hana-kisoi'. Its blossoms are positively monstrous, almost a foot wide and six to eight inches deep, truly cabbage-sized. The buds grow to about six inches in length before opening and are fat and heavy. (This is when you should cut them for bouquets.)

This plant did not flourish for me until I moved it to the top of the low berm, where it has open sky and good drainage. I feed it rose food in the spring, water it when it is setting buds, and dress it with manure every other April. This year I counted thirty blossoms.

from midsummer on and attracts butterflies and bumble-bees. There are several similar echinaceas with minor differences in structure, but they are basically alike in habit. They seed around and interbreed avidly, so I can no longer find a white or a deep pink one—they are all a soft rose. All summer long their central cones grow and grow, like Pinocchio's nose, and I leave them to catch snow caps in the winter.

Rudbeckia fulgida 'Goldsturm' is a daisy-form just as active for me, enough so that I dig out many plantlets in early summer and pot them up for plant sales, but I still love the accent of a thick clump of these very large yellow, black-centered daisy flowers amid the daylilies. *R. triloba*, the branched coneflower, sets so many seeds that I am not sure whether it is a perennial, as it comes up every year in an ever-widening area. I am never without it, and I enjoy the way its small black-eyed Susans space themselves on their stiff stems, up to four feet tall, to form a large but airy bank. In some years I have had to lift shovels full of baby plants to repot or give away. Other years are less productive.

A billowing, tall daisy-bloomer that has become very popular lately is *Boltonia asteroides*. It has small daisies, pink ones or white ones, and while it grows to six or seven feet tall it does not generally tower in the garden, because it flops. The boltonia needs bracing with branches poked firmly into the soil around it (the British call these "pea stakes"). Like *Gypsophila paniculata*, baby's breath, boltonias make a pleasant, light cloud of background lace for other plants. I am certain they will be subjected to a good pruning in June!

Intermediate Filler Plants

The smaller eupatoriums, with their large plates of fuzzy rose-colored blooms, are beautiful accent plants, but I think they need more sun than I can give them. I have tried *Eupatorium purpureum*, a two-foot-tall border plant with

lovely ageratum-blue flowers, and have not been able to bring it through a winter. I must try again, now that I have a garden in more sun, especially with the newer variety *E. rugosum* 'Chocolate', which has rich, dark leaves and the flat white blossom heads of the species, and reaches a comfortable two feet tall here, though listed as four feet.

Heucheras are small, compact plants, with thin, airy stems raising delicate bells high above their mounds of pretty leaves, earning them the name "coralbells." The flowers have no equal for delicacy and beauty, in my estimation. The ones to buy for blossom are legion, and all are delightful in white, pale to deep pink, and even fiery red. Any of them throw flowers that, dainty as they are, show up across the garden, bringing a lightness and delicacy no other plant can give, and if they are deadheaded they will bloom all summer long.

But it is the leaves which have sparked the latest breeding mania. Named cultivars are available in rich chocolates, reds, purples, copper, and pewter, with white, red, and even near-black variegations. Most heucheras take a small amount of shade but do best in full sun, with lots of humus and very good drainage. Those grown more for foliage will take a half-day of shade and look better for it, as sun can burn the leaf edges. These are good leaf-interest plants for groundcover around peonies, daylilies, and small trees or shrubs.

Heuchera 'Velvet Knight' has a dark, felty look that is wonderful with bronze ajugas, maidenhair ferns, and the winey cups of poppy mallows. For another effect, I have set these dark beauties among *Lysimachia nummularia* 'Aurea', the golden creeping Jenny, with *Corydalis lutea* and its pale yellow blossoms. Heucheras also hold their own with hybrid lamiums, tiarellas, pulmonarias, and even sweet woodruff, in nearly endless mix-and-match groundcover combinations.

In a hybrid between heuchera and tiarella, a new plant called heucherella has been bred that has delicate, feathery plumes of bell-like flowers, a perfect blend of coral bells and foam flowers. These lovely plants need loamy soil and good drainage, and in my garden they seem to need more light than the tiarellas. This is a dainty, close-up feature, worth the effort of moving it around a few times to find its ideal location. It deserves star billing, someplace where it isn't swamped by greedier plants.

Some small plants can take a lot of competition, and in fact look the better for it. I enjoy setting various kinds along path edges in such a way that they lap over the path and snuggle into one another in natural profusion. It is lovely to hear a visitor say, "Oh, it's marvelous how you did that!"—but I always have to confess that those great effects are mostly just happy accidents from letting good plants duke it out among themselves.

Dependable Staples

The geraniums provide an almost never-ending variety of attractive, durable plants for sunny borders, and some thrive in part shade. I grow six or seven varieties, plus the wild one, *Geranium maculatum*, which shows its pink flowers in our woods and has seeded into the shadiest gardens. *G. macrorrhizum* is perhaps my most visible one: a staunch, bushy border plant, a bit over a foot tall, with good pink blooms and minty-scented foliage. These plants have large stolons that reach out along the ground and root where they touch down, sending up new plants. From one plant, having divided it infinitely and given away a hundred babies, I now have a ten-foot curving swath of the original pink "old big-foot" to set off the smaller catmint, *Nepeta mussinii*, which puts out its blue fluff of bloom at the same time. The pink pokers of *Persicaria bistorta* are nice accents behind this border, and there are old clumps of monarda and iris that come along later, when the geraniums are quietly pretty in their

Top: White-blooming plants always light up the garden. Too often, buyers look only for the more colorful heuchera, believing that the white-blooming ones are dull. *Heuchera* 'White Marble' is not dull at all, but as bright and soft as a true lace veil, and about two feet tall. I like these plants at the foreground, where their small flowers form such semitransparent screens.

Bottom: *Heuchera* 'Pewter Veil' lays a cool pattern amid the greens of summer. There are many such new hybrid heucheras in amazing color combinations, most with extra-large leaves and long stems, making genuine design statements in the border. Their effect is mostly in their leaf patterns, as the blooms are small and neutral in color, though, like all heuchera blossoms, they always add a "dotted swiss" effect that lightens the garden mix.

Page 128 : *Geranium himalayense* 'Gravetye' satisfies that need for blue in the garden with a long-lasting show of large, striated true-blue blossoms held in a closely formed mass. Its sturdy stems do not creep and flop like those of *G*. 'Johnson's Blue', but make a full, well-shaped mound. This is a fine plant for the side of a brick walk and a great companion for Siberian irises and daylilies of any color.

foliage, turning soft shades of greenish-bronzy-red in fall. All of this with *Magnolia* 'Betty' and a Nanking cherry.

A new cultivar of this stolonizing geranium is *Geranium macrorrhizum* 'Bevan's Variety', which has deep magenta flowers with red sepals—stunning! I am searching for a place to put one.

G. clarkei 'Kashmir White' is a midsized plant, with true white blossoms and lighter green leaves. *G.* 'Johnson's Blue' has honestly deep-blue flowers, is good-sized and very floriferous, and if I had not found *G. himalayense* 'Gravetye', I would think 'Johnson's Blue' the best of the blues. The difference is mostly in habit: 'Gravetye' is much more tidy than 'Johnson's Blue' and has bigger blossoms almost the same color, but in a well-rounded clump rather than a sprawling heap. I still keep them both, and I deadhead them with shears after blooming, often getting late blooms.

G. sanguineum 'Lancastriense' is a much lower-growing, daintier specimen at four inches, with pale pink blooms that come all summer. *G. psilostemon* is a four-footer, with the deepest, hottest magenta blossoms, each with a black heart. I have not been able to make this one happy. A tiny border variety with similar black-hearted magenta blooms is *G. cinereum subcaulescens*, and the little flowers of the more sprawling *G. hybrida* 'Ann Folkard' are the same intense shade. I have her in the scree berm, where she can wander through small plants, lighting them up with her rich little blossoms. One of my other favorites is a low, spreading variety with good-sized carmine red blooms at about eight inches high: *G. sanguineum* 'John Elsley'. This one spreads thickly, and discourages other mat-formers in its vicinity, but it is gorgeous in bloom.

I could go on and on, but you get the geranium idea. Do not garden without these reliable, charming plants, which do so much to fill in the garden with good leaf quality and

blossoms in so many adaptable sizes and colors. Most of them work in sun or part-shade and are easy of culture, multiplying reliably, and probably requiring only good drainage. They all seem to be quite drought-hardy. You will find a long list of varieties described in catalogs and offered at your favorite nursery.

Catmints come in several useful sizes too, the largest I know of, at about two to three feet, being *Nepeta x faassenii* 'Six Hills Giant'. These and the smaller cultivars, *N. mussinii*, for one, bring the best soft blue flowers of the garden in nicely scented fluffy clumps. They make good borders for roses, salvias, and other leggy plants. As fillers and softeners they are right up there with the geraniums for usefulness. Cats like them all right, but not the way they like the wild catmint. I have seen my old cat, Claude, walk along the top rail of the fence in July, casually hook a paw around the blossoming tip of the tall wild catmint, eat about three inches of it, and then go bonkers, climbing the neighbor's clothesline post and cavorting like a kitten. A long nap always followed such behavior.

Geranium macrorrhizum, which I call "old bigfoot" because of its thick, surface-crawling, rooting stolons, is a reliable, rather coarse groundcover, with the added feature of really pretty pink bloom in late spring. It travels in dense colonies, each plant sending out its stolons across the surface to root down in a tangle. It never invades the lawn, but spends its energy thickening up and gradually extending the clump in a circular shape. I had to cut and move roots out along the front edge to form this linear border. One of the bonuses of handling this plant is its strong citrus-mint odor, which seems clean and medicinal to me.

Persicaria bistorta, which used to be called *Polygonum*, raises its pale pink pokers behind the geranium for a charming combination. This bit of lawn border was always difficult and weedy. Nothing wanted to grow there; I tried campanulas, large and small, foxgloves, irises, daylilies, and even hollyhocks. There was just not enough sun. Now these two tough, hardy plants make the area look good all summer long, even after blooming.

I love bergenia for its lustrous, plentiful leaves, which turn shades of bronze-red-green in fall and last all winter. A patch of bergenia in the border enriches any planting, and it is remarkably undemanding of soil or conditions. Yes, there are dead brown leaves to cull in spring, but it does not take long to spruce up the bergenia border. From my experience, the blossoms do not happen until you have had the plants a few years, but when they do, they are a sight to behold.

Old "Pig-Squeak"

Bergenias will grow in everything from full sun to partial shade. Even before their rigid, heavy stalks send up their buds and flowers above the leaves, they are beautiful with everything. But I like them most for the leaves, some of which have nice ruddy tones to give a fresh look to the midsummer garden. To promote this freshness, you will have to do some judicious cutting-out of browned leaves in spring and whenever else they appear.

These plants look as though they need to grow in a swamp, but in fact they take a good bit of drought and still look good; it's something in the structure of the leaves, which actually are so glossy that when rubbed together they make a little squealing noise, like sneakers on a tennis court. English children call them pig-squeak.

You may have bergenias with blossoms in all shades of red, rose, cream, and white, depending on variety. The sturdy bloom stalks shoot up in late spring bearing showy heads of bloom. Mine are the old-fashioned *Bergenia cordifolia* in a deep rose color; *B. c.* 'Bressingham White' has blossoms that start out pink, then turn pure white on red stems. You will find many others in catalogs and local nurseries.

Pretty Pests

Where I have the best southern exposure I leave a few of the ubiquitous *Oenothera fruticosa*, the evening primrose, for their rich yellow color. I keep them in spite of their ability to easily populate my entire garden, in fact, my entire city block, if I let them get out of hand, yet they are so cheerful and sweet that I need some.

But it is the large, papery-white flowers of *O. speciosa* which attract the most attention; the first flowers, for a week or two, can be almost three inches wide, with poppy-like tissue-papery petals, and the show is magnificent. Casual passersby often ask me whether it is a kind of poppy. This variety is also a spreader, and must be kept within bounds by pulling up some of the shallow-rooted clumps every spring. *O. s.* 'Siskiyou' is a pink form, with two-inch silvery-pink blossoms. I have not successfully grown a pink one in my garden. They are less dependable here, I think, than the others. All of them spread, yet they are all worth growing. The spreading can be controlled with attention every other year or so.

A Native Charmer

Liatris was first familiar to me as a roadside weed, which we called blazing star, that grew in the sand along the north-south highways we used to take to the lake in late summer. There, they made good-sized colonies, each plant with its several spikes of soft purple-pink on leafy stems. In my garden, *Liatris spicata* 'Kobold', a dwarf variety at about eighteen inches, has grown into a wide clump and been divided numerous times. There are several other purple varieties, some hybridized, but most native to some part of the country. Most *L. s.* is twenty-four to thirty inches tall. *L. scariosa* 'White Spires' makes a pure white exclamation point in the fall garden of a friend, who has a hospitable stony hillside.

As you might guess, this is another good subject for benign neglect. Don't fuss over it. Put it where you don't water or fertilize and where it gets hot, full sun, and when you next look at it, it will be big enough to divide. It has crisp, chunky roots, and it is hard to dig without some of them breaking. I forked into it accidentally one spring, as it is very late to show green. I was distraught, as I found I had five pieces of potato-white root. I hastily planted them all, in different places. Whoa! Every one came up and thrived.

Fall-Blooming Beauties

Japanese anemones are late-blooming tall plants that have a deceptively fragile appearance. Their foliage, deep green and somewhat ferny like heavier astilbes, is only about two feet high most of the summer; then four-foot stems rise, winged with a few leaves, and send out dozens of round buds that open in mid-September. They will take some shade but love morning sunlight. Although there are several delicious types, I grow only *Anemone vitifolia* 'Robustissima', the only one of a larger trial to survive the winters in my old, crowded beds. *A. x hybrida* 'Bressingham Glow'

PHOTOGRAPH BY TOM COTTINGTON

The fall show of asters is eagerly awaited here, compensating greatly for the loss of daylily blossoms. *Aster novae-angliae* 'Alma Potschke' is my favorite tall one because of its rich, deep pink color and because it does not need staking. In the years that I have not cut it back in June, it still stands well and makes lots of bloom. If I remember to cut back about a third to a half before July first, I get much more blossom and on shorter and sturdier stems.

would be a nice addition now that I have reworked that bed; it is a deep, rich pink.

A gorgeous white, *A. x h.* 'Honorine Jobert', is said to be equally hardy here, and it gives additional height, with pristine white blossoms; I may have to try that one again. The distinctive green globe centers of all the anemone blossoms are so effective in the white kinds.

For real excitement in the fall I turn to New England

and Belgian asters. My favorite New England is *Aster novae-angliae* 'Alma Potschke', a stunning hot pink. Although usually four feet tall, it does not need staking. I have a ditch-grown purple variety for companion and a hybrid they have made between them, a rose-purple one. When you see asters in the wild, you will note that they love ditches. Let that be a clue: water gathers in ditches. These plants flourish with a good supply of moisture. I have to water all of mine deeply as they grow to bloom size. The lower half of their stems sometimes need to be stripped of brown leaves if they have gotten too dry.

Asters also respond well to cutting back; they stand straighter and do not display such length of shabby stem (an aster failing). I cut the entire clump down to about half in June. The plants respond with a quick flush of leafy growth, then bloom twice as heavily in September on plants short enough not to need staking.

Companion Plantings

It is important to follow through on the garden's activity during the entire season so there will be companion plants for each phase. In fall, for instance, I face down the New England asters with mounds of Belgian asters. The *A. novi-belgii* hybrids are delightful low cushions of color, with solid masses of single daisy-blossoms that give lovely colorful cushion effects to borders, curbs, and sidewalks beginning in September. The cultivars *A. n.* 'Professor Von Kippenburg', 'Red Star', and 'Blue Opal' are just some of them. 'Purple Dome' is a deep purple, and 'Winston Churchill' is a stunning ruby-pink dwarf with large flowers. These all do well at the extreme front of the border. With richly colored late daylilies (try hot orange!) and the taller red, purple, and pink asters and chrysanthemums behind them, they give the garden a glorious late burst of color.

More Variety Than You Think

Veronicas come in many sizes, in blues, pinks, or white, with cultivars such as *Veronica spicata* 'Icicle', 'Blue Charm', 'Blue Peter', and 'Midnight', all promising dependable growth and color. 'Sunny Border Blue' makes a vigorous, thick clump about twenty inches high and wide for me, and therefore too greedy for my small garden spaces, though I have saved one plant for show. Its leaves are deep glossy green and the flower spikes a nice blue. If you have the room, it will give you the effect of a blue-flowering shrub by June. One groundcover type, *V. prostrata* 'Heavenly Blue' sends up a myriad of tiny five-inch spikes of just that color.

There are prostrate veronicas that I will describe later, as they are perfect for a gritty scree garden or a dry border.

Dry-Garden Plants

Sedums are the workhorses of the dry sunny border. Everyone knows *Sedum* 'Autumn Joy', with its soft brown-red blossoms. In my garden it is an imposing twenty-four inches tall and even wider. I would not be without it, but I would never have it as my only tall sedum. It is a sterile plant, and butterflies do not use it; the look of the more common *S.* 'Brilliant', with its pink fuzzy bloom plate alive with butterflies, is too nostalgic for me. It reminds me of the small-town gardens of my childhood.

Now *S.* 'Vera Jameson' has come along, with blue-purplish leaves and mauve blossoms, in a somewhat smaller size and more relaxed form, plus *S.* 'Atropurpurea', with its deep chocolate-purple leaves and mauve flowers, standing well over two feet tall, and the massive *S.* 'Matrona', with bluish-green leaves and rosy bloom, so that I have a wonderful play of color and size in the background of the curbside scree garden in late summer. I also have a white-variegated one, *S. alboroseum* 'Mediovariegatum', about a foot tall, which has creamy leaves bearing just a touch of green edge, and pale pink blooms, for a very different look in another border. I have to cut out and remove some of the reverted plain green-leaved stems once in a while, which I plant elsewhere.

There are also creeping sedums, of course, with white, yellow, pink, or red flowers, and I have tucked as many as possible into the gravelly sand of the front berm. Of the spreading, low-growing sedums, *S. acre* is the most floriferous, forming a sheet of yellow in bloom for two weeks in late May. *S. kamtschaticum* is even more interesting to me because of the russet coloration that undershades the yellow and persists when the yellow flowers are gone. Each of these gobbles up space and must be watched lest it overwhelm delicate alpines.

The sempervivums, or hens and chicks, may be the most popular plants in my curbside garden, and not only with children. I have several varieties, some red, some green, some wooly-white, and all thrive in fat rosettes in cracks between stones. In one pitted rock I have set tiny ones, each in a mere thimbleful of dirt, and some of them proceed to turn out a miniature family of "chicks" year after year. An occasional tower of bloom stem rises from one of the rosettes. These and other succulents create variety and beauty in waste places, with absolutely no care except a bit of tidying up. They are necessary with rocks and pebbles. Look for them.

We all know *Gypsophila paniculata*, baby's breath, though I think most of us who try to grow it have given up on its sprawling, ungrateful form, which has to be staked and girdled with string. But there are tiny, creeping ones that would charm anyone. I have *G. repens* 'Pink Festival' in the stony sand berm, where it spreads its flat fingers and covers them with tiny pink blossoms for a long time in midsummer. The flowers are just as ethereal as the florist's kind,

and set off other plants equally well, but in a different way.

Several clumps of a pink armeria, or thrift, occupy that part of the sand berm where the gypsophila creeps, and to fill out the theme I have found a rich pink double portulaca, which seeds true, for this spot. In May and June, therefore, before the *Opuntia compressa* cactus puts out its yellow poppies, I have a pink show that won't quit, lovely against pebbles and blue-green foliage.

The most ephemeral spring accents in this garden are the *Anemone pulsatilla*, those soft lavender flowers that we used to call crocuses when we gathered them from the fields to put on the altar at Easter time. Their furry stems, and later their smoky seed heads, always take me back to those days. So do the birdsfoot violets popping up from their finely divided leaves here and there among this grouping. Those are reminders of days on my grandfather's farm in the midst of a sandy prairie full of lupines, violets, and sandburs, where I walked (carefully!) as a little girl. *Opuntia compressa* cactuses grew in this prairie; that's where I got mine.

Tucked into several odd corners of the sandy garden is *Ruellia humilis*, the so-called wild petunia. It isn't a petunia relative at all, of course, but its flowers do look like small versions of them. A bushy little trailing plant, it is never really evident until some morning in June when I go out and find its frail purple flowers trailing all down the rocks in the sunniest spots, some already faded and dropped. After that a mass of "petunias" continues most of the season, finishing with russet-toned seed pods in fall.

A Few Herbs in the Sand

There are herbs that do very well in the well-drained sandy scree, and the best of them in my garden is *Lavendula* 'Hidcote'. I have been so happy to at last bring this plant through our winters and to discover that drainage is defi-

Right: Lavender is one of those plants I always knew I must have. The scent is nostalgic: clean and pure and warm. I add dried lavender blossoms to hot green tea for a spirit boost in gray winter weather and use lavender oil as a rub for headaches.

Lavender is reliable in Zone 4, but only if it has excellent, sharp drainage. *Lavendula* 'Hidcote' grows here in a mix of one part sharp sand, one part pea gravel, and one part rice hulls. I cut it back to a couple of inches in early spring to keep it in shape; otherwise, it will have one or two long, straggly branches and a cluster of small growth. Where you do not have room to create a sandy berm, raise the planting bed and set lavender in a mix of gritty sand in the hole. Adding a sand mulch raised to about two inches or so in late fall will save the crown of the plant through the wettest winter.

Opposiste: *Liatris spicata* 'Kobold' is a shorter form of this late-blooming prairie plant, which makes thick clumps of blazing stars in just a few years. It is easy to divide; simply cut a chunk of the crispy root and stick it into poor, sandy soil. Fall is the best time to divide it, mostly because you cannot find it in early spring; it sprouts late. Be certain to mark the location so you will not accidentally dig out a clump before its shoots break the surface.

nitely the answer. Now, just by walking past and brushing near this healthy plant, I can bring out the aroma best-loved in the entire world.

The other herb I like to grow here is sage—both plain *Salvia officinalis* and *S. o.* 'Tricolor', which has a clear pink-and-cream variegation on its sage-green leaves. I use the leaves fresh for tea, stuffing, or garnish, sometimes frying them in olive oil to decorate risotto or grilled fish. You must try this! Sage is wonderful in applesauce, too. I use it fresh until the threat of a really deep snowfall, when I turn to my dried store of leaves. I dry sage leaves simply by cutting stems in late summer and hanging them in the shady porch until they are crisp, when I bottle them or seal them in plastic baggies.

Thymus citriodorus, lemon thyme, nestles between rocks in this fast-draining environment, and its true lemon flavor is another favorite for cooking.

Creeping thyme, *T. serpyllum*, would love to get in there too, but it swarms over everything, so I confine it to another place on the curb where it can flow unobstructed.

Gilia aggregata or Ipomopsis aggregata, whichever you call this unusual plant, is known as skyrocket in its native habitat, the high plains of western North America. Although a perennial, it behaves in the Midwest as a biennial, sending up many hardy seedlings every spring, which never grow more than about six inches tall. They form short, almost ferny humps the first summer, and the following spring shoot up to three or four feet, where they open their red firecrackers slowly, lasting about two weeks.

One prairie plant, which has come to my garden from a friend, is so spectacular that I was startled one evening to see headlights as a driver maneuvered his truck around to shine them on the curbside scree garden to show his wife the tower of fiery blossoms he had seen the day before. The plant is *Ipomopsis rubra,* also known as *Gilia rubra,* which by rights does not belong in this discussion at all because it is a biennial in this climate, though its seedlings survive. It is a high plains Colorado native. In its first season, gilia is a hairy little dwarf, humped about three or four inches high and fluffy, with divided, thread-thin leaves. In its second year, it elongates into a three- to four-foot thread-leaved spike, most of which is studded with firecracker-red tubular blossoms for weeks near the end of summer. It really is a show worth revisiting!

Cactus

Many cactus varieties will grow in cold zones, but I rely mainly on a native prickly pear, *Opuntia compressa.* Its semi-double yellow blossoms crowd its flat pads, and I can usually count on them for a Fourth-of-July appearance. The plants are sited in the grit garden at the curb, under open sky, shaded by trees only for a couple of hours in late afternoon. It would perhaps be happier without even that shade, but it blooms well.

Specialty catalogs list other hardy kinds, and I have friends who grow an abundance of them, with blooms from orange through bright red and magenta. They are best grown in raised, gritty beds and really constant sun, which of course I cannot provide.

PHOTOGRAPH BY TOM COTTINGTON

Opuntia compressa, the prickly pear cactus, is native to Wisconsin's sandy prairies. In full sun and a well-drained bed, my patch flowers prolifically on or about the Fourth of July every summer and continues for at least two weeks. The edible fruits that form after bloom are tasty, but prickly; I made jam once only, and have not thought it worthwhile to do so again. I keep the patch in bounds by cutting out heavily overlapping clumps to give away to friends.

Try Some Rare Alpines

One cannot have a patch of well-drained sunny garden without being tempted at some point to try to grow at least a few of the true rock garden plants, the alpines. These are a specialist's study, and I am a mere dabbler, but by talking with local rock gardeners and asking for information about "easy" alpines, I became acquainted with some of these close-up plants. Some of them are so tiny that they must be put in holes in rocks, or in pots or troughs set into the garden. I like best those that have a bit more presence, or those that form mats.

Among the best are the veronicas, which, as I have said, surprised me with several creeping, low-blooming cultivars for alpine conditions. One of the lowest growing, and my fa-vorite, is *Veronica liwanensis,* Turkish speedwell. It spreads out at two inches high, covering itself with sky-blue flowers in spring and maintaining its ruglike form with shining green foliage and sporadic bloom for the rest of the summer.

If you have the space and like rug-spreaders, one of the nicest of the silver-gray velvet kinds is *Artemisia stellerana* 'Silver Brocade', at six inches or less in height. I cut off the six-inch stems of white bloom as fast as it browns, to show off the leaves.

An even more tempting plushy leaf is found on *Tanace-tum vulgare* 'Crispum', a creeping tansy that spreads out much lower here than the eighteen-inch height it is supposed to reach. It does not bloom for me, and so maintains its green-silver furry presence all summer. It really takes up room, but it

Top: *Lewisia cotyledon* is small but stunning, with its cream-pink-gold coloration and sharply striped appearance. The light borders on the petals are clear and distinct, making each small plant highly visible

These plants grow from rosettes of leaves that need to be rooted in some humus but that like to have deep collars of sandy gravel to keep them from rotting in the wet. I find they appreciate the shade from nearby small plants or large rocks. They also need to be watered occasionally in times of serious drought.

Bottom: The scree garden, with full sun and southern exposure, is always a quilt of color and texture: rock, sand, gravel, blossom, and leaf. Xeric plants survive in the sharply draining mix, and species tulip bulbs repeat every spring. In May, *Androsache lanuginosa*, with its many primula-like blooms in soft pink, is nicely set off by *Veronica liwanensis*, a spreading two-inch mat of tiny, upfacing, bright blue flowers.

doesn't mind being cut back. What it does mind is rain; an unusually wet year will cause it to rot out and disappear.

Penstemons, the beardtongues, like sharp drainage, and come in all sizes from two inches to three feet. *Penstemon barbatus* is tallest, with bright red two-lipped flowers, and *P. grandiflorus* has large, lilac-pink blooms. The alpine *P. fruticosus* 'Purple Haze' makes a mat about eight inches tall by about two feet wide, flowering thickly with two-toned lavender-purple flowers. All are short-lived.

For a small plant with real character, *Acantholimon hohenackeri,* prickly dianthus, can't be beat. For me it is about four inches high, spreading to about one foot, and set with sharp prickles close together. When it puts out its slightly taller stems of teeny pink bloom and finishes with whitish seed capsules, it rather spoils the pincushion effect, but it is always quite lovely.

Lewisias grow in the gritty berm too, though they need special care. *Lewisia cotyledon* is the variety I find in a local nursery. From a small rosette of elongated oval leaves, slender stems raise the most beautiful full heads of small, round, single flowers of pink or peach, with candy-striped petals, which stay in bloom for a long time. They are not easy to please. Their most stringent requirement seems to be perfectly sharp drainage, though they want to be fed and watered during summer dry spells, as long as the water is not allowed to stand on leaves or crown. I think they like afternoon shade, too, or at least a spot near a cool rock.

One garden writer describes filling a strawberry jar with a fast-draining mix similar to that I used in the berm and planting it with *L. cotyledon*, where it blooms like mad every spring but then looks dreary the rest of the year. I set mine in small pockets of compost packed in the gritty sand berm and bring collars of pea gravel up under their leaves. I like to grow them where other plants will surround and flower after them.

(Yes, they are named for Meriwether Lewis, as the plant was discovered and named on the Lewis and Clark Expedition.)

A similar treatment has worked for *Androsace lanuginosa*, which grows from a neat mound of green rosettes with cobwebby centers and sends up a truly primula-like profusion of small pink flowers in May. This plant spreads gently and sends outshoots all around to colonize quite a patch of garden. It couldn't be more welcome.

Geranium cinereum subcaulescens is a little alpine charmer that makes a small, well-contained clump in the scree bed, showing true pink blossoms in early summer and reddish-tinted stems and leaves as the season rolls on.

In this area, as well, I have put many small, creeping varieties of sedum, draba, mazus, arabis, and campanula. The alpine qualities of these plants, so reduced in size, include a tendency to be xeric; that is, not requiring frequent watering. The overall effect of this garden is that of a softly colored patchwork quilt, changing color with passing phases of bloom, but basically lovely for the leaf tones against the sand and pebbles. But for lack of space, I could add dozens of other plants to enhance this bed; this is an exciting branch of gardening. I foresee that I will be expanding the scree berm soon.

Some Old Friends Come in New Dresses

Achillea is now available in so many cultivars, sizes, and colors that it must not be left out of any sunny garden. If you have tried some form of it and had trouble with its becoming sparse and lax, that's not because it's hard to grow but because you have given it too rich a diet or perhaps not given it full sun. Starve it in sand and gravel, in full sun, and it will feather out into lovely drifts: white, cream, yellow, pink, cinnamon, rust, rose, red—in shades that go with everything. There is no plant whose blooms look better with its leaves:

PHOTOGRAPH BY TOM COTTINGTON

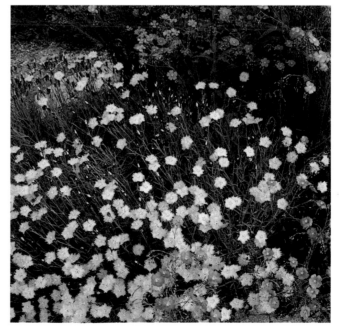

Top: *Achillea tomentosa* 'Aurea' forms a low, creeping, solid mat of scented, wooly foliage, and sends up a myriad of rich, yellow yarrow blossoms on eight-inch stems in July. With the spent blooms cut back, it forms an attractive bluish-green carpet in the sand garden for the rest of the season.

This plant is hardy in the coldest winters and tolerates being deeply covered with snow at curbside. In two or three years it may crowd small, delicate things such as lewisias and androsaces; I simply pull some loose and cut it away from them. This is never a disposal problem, as rock gardening friends love to receive cuttings.

Bottom: *Dianthus* 'Bath's Pink' is not only the most reliable of its family in this part of the world but also one of the prettiest, I think. It blooms at curbside, surrounded by blue flax. Together they make a gentle but telling combination in bloom. Both love the dry, unfertilized conditions in gritty sand, where they rarely get watered.

Fragaria 'Pink Panda' is a non-fruiting strawberry that extends its runners flat along the ground and opens large, pink, single-rose blossoms all along their length. The plants never stand more than about three or four inches high and mingle nicely with other low plants and groundcovers, in sun or half-shade. The small purple blooms of *Viola labradorica* have seeded among them here in high, filtered shade.

ferny little gray-green leaves that have an antiseptic odor. It is perfect to set off the larger sedums, daylilies, coreopsis, chrysanthemums, and echinaceas that grow in the hottest sunny places. It also provides good places to hide tulip leaves as they age. There are also alpine varieties of achillea, which have ground-hugging gray foliage and send up white or yellow yarrow blossoms on short stems.

Allium senescens 'Glaucum', with its twisted, flattened, blue onionlike leaves, looks even better in the scree garden than it does by the driveway. When it blossoms, it revives the impression of the thrift that bloomed before it, though in a softer version of pink, and it lasts for several weeks.

Dianthus 'Bath's Pink' is positively the most dependable dianthus and the most hardy for me. It makes a glorious accent all summer, first with its broad cushion of blue spiky foliage, then with the airy forest of purplish exclamation-point buds, and then for at least two weeks with a one-foot-deep pillow of baby-girl pink blooms. I cut this back when the bloom is all done, right down to the low tops of the early foliage, because a fresh cushion of blue spikes will grow up to adorn the border path. *D. caesius* 'Tiny Rubies' is the only other dianthus I grow; it creeps down even the shady side of the front berm, sprinkling its small bright red dots everywhere, in between and around everything that grows, finally entangling itself in the *Myosotis alpestris*, the forget-me-not, which is positively rampant along the curved brick walk, making a sheet of the loveliest blue imaginable for a few weeks in late May and early June.

Pretty Creepers

I like small creeping things that blossom, even when they get into everything. *Fragaria* 'Pink Panda' is one. Its wide-open little single pink roses lie close to the ground on wandering vines. I do not cut the runners back, but maybe

Page 141: The creeping *Callirrhoe involucrata*, poppy mallow, has been a joy to me since the day I planted it, and it is noticed by every garden visitor. From a distance, its blossoms resemble those of a geranium, but it has a habit of laying out very long tendrils over the walk and over and under surrounding plants and of throwing out these marvelous little winey cups through the whole composition. It does this all summer long until frost, and it comes back safely every spring.

I love things that grow in such a way as to tie plant combinations together, literally and visually. These are not bothersome trailing vines, but merely sprawling, thin plants, and they add a richness to any mix. The odd, speckled orange flowers belong to *Belamcanda chinensis*, blackberry lily, which forms seed heads resembling blackberries. The young foliage of the annual red mint, perilla, is so perfect with callirrhoe that I leave it until it grows gawky. Then I pull it up.

that's just my "green tapestry" mentality. I let them infiltrate the bed.

Another pretty creeper is *Callirrhoe involucrata*, the poppy mallow, which throws its light runners up and out into the entire front garden on either side of the brick walk, frequently decorating the walk itself with its wine-colored mallow cups. It grows from a central plant with rather geranium-like leaves, but it can spread its thin runners three or four feet in all directions and blossom at their tips. I sometimes see the flowers at the tops of peony bushes or lily stems. I like it enormously.

A Non-Creeping Strawberry

Fragaria 'Fraises des Bois' is a much more polite strawberry; it does not run, and it produces fruit and white blossoms at the same time all summer long on the south side of the front berm. It has amazingly flavorful berries, fingertip-small; as few as five or six of them are enough to raise to gourmet status a big bowl of cornflakes. It is not to be disregarded as a border plant, either, as it divides easily and forms a long, neat, mounded row in a hurry.

Lots of Blue

Many of the campanulas are creepers, and some even form good, blossoming groundcover. The lower-growing forms, *Campanula carpatica*, *C. cochlearifolia*, *C. rotundifolia*, *C. poscharskyana*, and so on (and on!), are excellent for curb edges, berms, and sunny border fronts, and all are very easy to grow. My favorite local nursery listed twenty-four varieties of campanula in last year's catalog. All have more or less bell-shaped blooms, in shades of blue, though some face upward and open almost fully, some hang in tender little fairy bells, and some are almost closed. Some of these wide-ranging plants are creeping alpines and love the sparse con-

ditions in the gravel berm; some like the half-shade of the other borders.

I have *C. glomerata*, a greedy spreader, growing in one garden, and, though it tries hard to take over the whole space, nothing could induce me to eradicate it. It is simply the most intense, rich, purple-blue in the world; its globes of color, rising to about two feet or less, are necessary to the spirit at a certain time of year. When the upper globe turns shabby, I cut it off and watch a second globe of bloom come to life. The stems need to be cut all the way down after these fade, but I don't even mind that. It has to be thinned out every year; I have always been able to find friends who have waste sunny corners to fill with such a blue, so I dig plants to give away.

Some Spiky Accentss

Siberian irises have been hybridized extensively; some of their blooms are now almost as wide and flat as Japanese iris. There are more colors, too. The culture of these plants is simplicity itself. They like a well-prepared bed, of course, but are otherwise undemanding in the extreme. I do warn about attempting to pull out brown leaves with bare hands in fall, or even next spring: these fibers are tough! I had many a deep cut before I learned to use strong, sharp cutters and heavy gloves to remove old leaves. Siberians make substantial clumps, but do not really need to be divided unless you are out of room, or simply want more plants. When you do divide, you will absolutely have to dig the entire clump, and saw or chop it apart by main force.

I have six or eight varieties, chosen for color. None can be recommended above the others for anything besides color, or perhaps size of bloom, if that's important, but catalogs do an adequate job of helping you choose. I might suggest that the little *Iris siberica* 'Flight of Butterflies' is a must for its purple-veined falls, and 'Butter and Sugar' for the delicacy of its lemony colors, but then I would also have to talk about 'Sparkling Rose', 'Eric the Red', 'Gull's Wing', and 'Purple Velvet'.

Do grow Japanese iris if you have a moist, acid, organic soil; their blooms can be over eight inches wide, and their colors are glorious. I do wish I could grow them, but the better part of gardening is to remember the limits of both plants and gardener. These lovely plants would not like the conditions I have at present, and I would have to develop a special bed to accommodate them.

I do not have many bearded irises, either, and that is by choice as well, because I have so little full sun. I grow only one, an unnamed old purple variety that smells like grape juice and grows in a cleft between boulders, where it never attracts borers. I used to have many more. I do like them, but they are too prone to borers and consequent root rot in my too-shady location.

Some iris have more leaf than blossom interest. I. *pallida* 'Aurea-Variegata' has yellow-striped leaves and looks wonderful near chartreuse-leaved hostas, wherever they are grown in enough sun for the iris. I grow *I. p.* 'Albo-Variegata' for its white-edged upright leaves, which I like to place near white-blooming or white-leaved plants, such as *Geranium* x *cantabrigiense* 'Biokovo', *Dictamnus albus*, *Pulmonaria* 'Excalibur', *Lamium* 'White Nancy', or *Hosta* 'White Christmas'. The pale blue blossoms of pallida are nice, but I am never sad when it is time to cut them off. The foliage just grows and gets better looking all season.

The Ultimate Accent

I would be remiss if I did not call your attention to the grasses now so popular for full sun, because they do more than any one thing to bring a garden to life. When a garden

Top: The Siberian iris 'Butter and Sugar' is a breakthrough beauty that opens large blooms in June, with near-white standards and pale yellow falls and beards. Like all Siberians, it holds the blossoms high on stiff stalks amid slender iris foliage, which stays nice all season. *Clematis* 'Nellie Moser' backs it up with masses of bloom every summer, and Culver's root raises its tiered stems of leaves in preparation for the white spikes of bloom that will follow in July. Culver's root has since been moved to make room for climbing roses.

Bottom: An early arrival, following soon after the small bulbs in spring, is the dwarf *Iris* 'Gingerbread Man', a lovely form with odd coloring: warm brownish-orange petals and sky-blue beards. It is less than a foot tall and generous in its production of flowers. This is a good spreader, with shallow rhizomes that are easy to divide and separate. All it needs is good drainage and a prominent position in the front of the border, where its quiet coloration will show up well.

contains grasses, especially tall grasses, its composition is lightened and enhanced manyfold, and its overall design is clearer and more visible from a distance. *Miscanthus sinensis* 'Morning Light' and 'Variegata' are the best of the tall grasses, substantial enough for one plant to lighten a garden. Miscanthus needs room, all right, but will stay in a controllable clump and reward you for giving it space with a tall spray of leaves and six-foot feathery white plumes late in the season, and will go on to improve its looks with rosy-tan fall and winter foliage. Give it four feet of space for best effect. If you are fortunate enough to have the right place, an entire bed of their silky fronds makes an incomparable background. Many of us have no room for six-footers that require this much garden space, and I myself do not use many.

In the medium-sized range, I would have to say that *Pennisetum alopecuroides*, fountain grass, is my favorite grass, so far, for feathery, open effect. It has silvery, dark-seeded foxtails of bloom on a fountain of thin reedy stems from midsummer. It is nearly three feet tall, but I have used it effectively at the edge of a brick walk, at the front of the border, and I love the way it works as a sheer screen for the bulkier plants behind it. *P. a.* 'Little Bunny' is an eleven-inch miniature of this form and absolutely adorable.

Hakonechloa macra is a green, slightly bamboolike, twenty-four-inch clumper that will take part shade, but it is happy in the most sun I can give it. It has a cascading effect that is very interesting. But for the newest and daintiest of the midsized grasses, I recommend *Miscanthus* 'Bitsy Ben', a recently developed cultivar. It has all the best characteristics of the loveliest *Miscanthus* cultivars but takes up no more room than a small daylily. *Festuca glauca* is another small favorite; clumping at about a foot tall and as wide, it is a perfect blue accent for so many things in my sunniest spots: *Opuntia* cactuses, moss roses, thymes, and creeping campan-

ulas in particular. Blue oat grass, *Helictotrichon sempervirens*, will give you this blue-spiked effect in a two-foot version for a more substantial planting.

One or two tips on grass cultivation are important here. The first is cleanup: I do not like to cut back grasses in fall, because they are so beautiful in snow. Yet they must be cleaned up well before growth begins in spring, so I get out there as early as possible, March or April, and cut them cleanly to the ground, as soon as the snow melts. It is not, however, wise to divide them too early. Wait until there are new green blades growing before digging clumps to divide. For some reason, grasses divided before this crucial point do not survive.

As one newly come to grass gardening, I have to say that nothing has given me so much new appreciation for all my companion plants as the delicacy of grasses set among them. Do explore your options.

Sedges are lovely grassy additions to any planting, and some work in sun, some in shade. *Carex morowii temnolepis*, called silk tassel sedge, is a fine-textured, silver-striped variety that grows in an attractive small clump, a foot or so tall and wide, in a quite shady spot.

C. elata 'Aurea' is somewhat larger, and a good yellow, forming a waterfall accent with hostas and other shade plants. For a larger green sedge, try the shining green *C. pendula*, weeping sedge, a two-footer that works well in woodland borders from sun to partial shade.

Opposite: *Helictotrychon sempervivens,* **blue oat grass, is a welcome spray of blue at the very front of a sunny border in May, forming up earlier in the spring than many of the other grasses. It holds its own as the season progresses, too, growing tall stems with oat-like heads to lighten a garden filled with large-leaved perennials and colorful blooms.**

Bulbs for Interplanting

Only the sky can match the blues of Chionodoxa luciliae, Scilla siberica, *and* Iris reticulata,

while Iris danfordiae *and* Crocus ancyrensis *reflect the sun in tints of clear yellow and orange.*

And the rich creamy white of Crocus crysanthus *'Cream Beauty', the ice blue of* Crocus tommasinianus,

and the feathered purple of Crocus corsicus *are the colors of the moon and stars. These purest colors of the*

gardening year are seen in the high bright light of the April sun, as far up in the sky as it will be in September,

but shining through the yet-unfurnished branches of the trees with extraordinary intensity.

Joe Eck and Wayne Winterrowd, *A Year at North Hill: Four Seasons in a Vermont Garden*
Little, Brown, 1995

N ZONE 5 AND northward the season is short, as we all know, and most of us wish our gardens to provide a show for the entire six months between freezes. About the time our snow melts, we are nearly desperate for the sight of some bright color in the garden. We have had our deprivation. We want color now! Bulbs are really the only way to have very early color in the northern garden.

All bulbs need sun to bloom and will do very well in the most exposed places, but there are many bulbs you can tuck into your shade gardens. In doing so you are following nature; the spring-flowering bulbs are done blooming before the trees leaf out and obliterate the sun.

Never Enough Daffodils

The most all-around bulb for either a woodland or a sunny setting is the daffodil. Daffs are extremely adaptable, tolerating summer shade and more moisture than tulips. The bulbs and foliage are also disagreeable to animal browsers: deer, squirrels, voles, or whatever, so planting them is a good investment. The patches you plant will continue to increase year after year, filling in large areas more quickly than you expect. And such variety! Any size and type of bloom you may wish, for any given spot.

I plant the larger ones singly, nearly a foot deep and two feet apart in the woodsy beds, so that I get an open planting and soon have nicely spaced large clumps of the different kinds. Unless for some reason you absolutely must have a massive, close-blooming show the first year, do not succumb to the grower's advice that you plant your bulbs only four or five inches apart. If you do, in about two or three years you will have a tight mass of leaves without blooms, which will have to be dug up and divided. Good fertilization will delay this occurrence, but not for long. The smaller daffodils, such as the little species and wild forms, do need to be planted

more closely, of course.

If you do not care whether your blooms are grouped by type, are not choosy about varieties, and want a quick show, you may purchase naturalizing daffodils in collections at great bargains. I think this is fine for a situation in which the flowers are usually viewed from a little distance. I personally like mine grouped by type, in overlapping drifts. However you use them, you should order as many hundreds of daffodil bulbs, of as many kinds as you can handle and afford, and put them everywhere you need color in the spring. The sight of them blossoming in the bare woods is so cheering, you will buy hundreds more the next year, I guarantee. You will also become more discriminating and want some of the newest cultivars. The best bulb catalogs are full of so many exciting selections that you will never have enough.

The caution in all this is that daffodil and jonquil leaves, in fact all bulb leaves, must be left in place to ripen in order to feed the bulb for the next year's bloom. It is best not to braid them, or twist them in clumps, as they need sunlight and oxygen to convert their sugars to bulb energy. Hostas are perfect cover for bulb leaves, along with ferns, lady's mantles, astilbes, daylilies, epimediums, pachysandras, or any medium-height ground cover that makes dense foliage which will grow as the daffodils finish blooming. I plant bulbs in wide rings around large plants, about a foot from the plant roots, or scatter them through the groundcovers. Bulbs planted in groundcover might show some of their drying leaves sticking up above the cover, but these can be tucked behind and under leafy places. Bulb leaves must be left until they wilt and yellow, about eight weeks. Then remember that rotting leaves encourage slugs under hostas.

How to tell you my favorites? I don't even know that I should. I put so many daffs in when we came here over twenty years ago that they are all "oldies" now. Search good

Page 146: *Crocus chrysanthus* may be small, but it produces many blossoms per bulb, and its contribution only grows over the years, as animals do not eat it. This small bulb is good for dry shade under trees, and will naturalize well in grass, not causing a bit of fuss with its marrow leaves befor mowing time.

Page 149: A sweep of mixed daffodils reaches from the street to the back of the lot, and is carried in varying degrees throughout the entire landscape. It is basically a yellow palette, and I must admit that, as a rank beginner, I had rather longed for the more brilliant colors of massed tulips, with daffodils perhaps for accent. This is a lesson hard learned: tulips are temporary. You must depend upon the daffodil family for permanence, and use other bulbs for color.

PHOTOGRAPH BY TOM COTTINGTON

Top: 'Thalia' is one of the *triandrus* daffodils that produces more than one bloom per stem. It is a delicate, small bloom, with a slender trumpet and a great fragrance. 'Thalia' blooms mid-to-late in the daffodil season, after the eaerliest ones, but while there are still plenty of others for company.

Bottom: *Narcisssus* **'Peeping Tom'** is always my favorite for a week or so in spring, as it blooms with the first crocuses. It lasts a long, long, time, too, keeping its fresh, perky stance for close to three weeks.

catalogs for new introductions! I like whites in the distance, and both the big, creamy old *Narcissus* 'Mt. Hood' and the pale yellow-cupped 'Ice Follies' show up well. 'Mrs. R.O. Backhouse' was my first pink trumpet, and she is still lovely late in May, especially near white ones. Yellow and orange seem to put her at a disadvantage. 'Salome' is my only other pink, and its long cups are coral pink, rimmed gold. Both of these rosy ladies open almost cream-yellow and turn color after a few days.

Later blooming daffodils are *N. poeticus*, a fresh-faced type, usually with a small yellow-green cup and purest white petal collar. *N. p.* 'Pheasant's Eye' has a distinctive disc-shaped cup rimmed with red and eyed with gold and green. Of the *triandrus* type, my favorite is the late-blooming 'Thalia', with its several fragrant winged white blossoms on each stem. 'Thalia' is tolerant of part shade and some moisture. 'Hawera', a miniature with multiple pendant tiny yellow flowers, needs more sun and better drainage.

The *cyclamineus* daffodils are so adorable in bloom, and so petite, that I swerve close to the hated adjective cute. One of the most appealing, 'Peeping Tom', has its small petals back-swept enough from the long, slender trumpet that it actually gives the impression of "peeking" out. 'Jack Snipe' is a dainty bicolor, with lightly swept-back white petals and lemon-yellow crowns. Both of these need good drainage and some sun to thrive. For me they multiply in nice little clumps, living for years. I do not grow these in shade.

Miniature Daffodils

And we haven't even touched upon the miniature species! Do look into these little wild daffodil bulbs, especially if you have a scree or rock garden. They are best viewed in rather bare surroundings, and up close, as in a raised bed where you can really keep track of them. Learn

Every year the front berm is glorious with the progeny of the miniature daffodil bulbs I planted the first fall. *Narcissus triandrus* 'Ice Wings' presents all this bloom where three bulbs were set five years ago. *Primula acaulis* and forget-me-nots are common, rock-hardy companions in perfect scale to set off small bulb plants. The red fronds of *Paeonia suffruticosa* rise and gradually open behind the flowers, and the bulb blossoms last until they are backed by ruddy peony leaves.

where each of them came from, so you can provide optimum conditions. I would caution, right at the start, that most of the very small species daffodils, which often originate in high mountains with no forest cover, do not lend themselves to woodland planting; they do not like either the summer shade or the year-round moisture. Mostly, they have not liked my normal soil, either, even in full sun. The conditions they like best include the scree mix I discuss elsewhere, mounded high, and a good, hot, baking summer. None of them will be happy in a wet situation, especially one that produces ice in winter around the bulbs. They will die. You might think you are doing them a favor by creating a rich, humusy soil, but in nature these small bulbs are mostly found in gravelly, well-drained mountain pastures, where they have lots of snow cover, moist conditions (from snow melt) just before and at bloom time, and nice dry, sunny summers. I have been setting species daffodil bulbs in little pockets of compost in the sandy berm at the street side and trying not to water there in summer. I also have them on the sloping sides of a somewhat shadier berm.

Discouraging Animal Pests

First, a short cultural note: nearly every variety of the following bulbs is considered tasty by some form of wildlife. You will read dozens of suggestions for keeping them away: animal or human hair in nylon stockings, bars of soap, cayenne pepper, wire netting, and on and on. They may all work, for at least some part of the problem. Recently I read a serious account of using an outdoor radio that had a heat-sensitive switch, and began to play music when an animal walked into range, such as a deer or a raccoon. According to the writer, this treatment really scares animals away.

My simpler method has worked very well to date: dried blood meal sprinkled over freshly planted bulbs to keep squirrels from digging them up, and around the new shoots in spring to keep deer and rabbits from eating them.

The Little Bulbs

Drifts of hundreds of snowdrops, squills, crocuses, puschkinia, and glory-of-the-snow are excellent for damp woodland conditions, especially in good humus. The very best of these, to my taste, is *Galanthus nivalis*, the common snowdrop, because its paired white bells come so early while the earth is still frosty, and because most years there is not even any green grass to set them off. Nothing else looks like spring, but suddenly I know it's on the way. Catalogs list several kinds of galanthuses, including a beautiful double *G. n.* 'Flore Pleno'.

As a suggestion, plant dense drifts of any of the small bulbs far back in the lawn; they will bloom before the paths are dry enough for you to walk out to visit them, so you need sheets of color. That will be before most plants, such as peonies and hostas, are up, and even before the earliest daffodils, so you can plant these little bulbs right above and around the larger bulbs and the roots of all your other plants.

Planting them right in the grass lawn is an option, depending upon how fussy you are about clean mowing and how early in the spring mowing begins. Bulb foliage needs to ripen, sometimes taking long enough that grass gets shaggy.

The Littlest Tulips

Species tulips, having such small foliage, are a great choice for small show places in sunny sites: in a raised bed, before a large boulder, on the scree slope, around a tree, along a path, anywhere their short stature can be seen and their lovely blossoms enjoyed, as long as it is dry in summer. I do not think there is one over six inches in height, and many are a mere two or three inches. Some of their blooms are not as miniature as their other parts, so you will be amused every spring by the large cups of bloom on such petite stalks, whose leaves are reduced often to ground-hugging wisps.

I plant these bulbs a bit more deeply than directions say, because I think the clumps last longer that way. Again, watch the catalog information carefully, as some of these little gems come from high mountains where they have lots of cold water and sharp drainage in spring, and a long, dry summer of sun and wind. These won't like mulchy conditions and constant dampness or shade, and will die if that's what you give them. Still, there are some, *Tulipa tarda* for one, that will thrive in woodland conditions and quite heavy soil, as long as they have drainage and a dry summer.

I am growing several kinds of species tulips and get my best results in the gritty berm. The small plants show up well there, having no competition, and receive the sharp drainage they love. *T. t.* 'Dasystemon' opens its creamy white petals widely into star-shapes revealing a yellow center, which, sprinkled along a bank, make a cheery sight in early May. *T. pulchella* 'Violacea' comes along later, with brilliant magenta blossoms in the more traditional tulip shape and a clean

Opposite: *Tulipa greigii* 'Pink Sensation' is a great spring spirit-lifter. Sometimes a closely planted bed of tulips is just the right thing for a certain spot. I am no devotee of successive mass plantings of tulips and annuals for color, however, and I do not dig up tulip bulbs at the end of their season. These are set between perennials and will be left to diminish over the next few years, though with a hopeful handful of bulb fertilizer, when they are done with each year's bloom.

Top: *Tulipa tarda* is one of those high-country species tulips which likes a dry summer and a cold winter. I try to give it these conditions in the scree bed and to keep it separated from any plants which need summer watering. There is no flower more cheerful, though on cloudy days it does not come out to brighten the garden but stays tightly closed.

This species produces many blossoms per bulb, and is also inclined to seed itself around, even as it mutiplies its original bulbs.

Bottom: *Tulipa bakeri* 'Lilac Wonder' opens its pale stars in the gravel of the sandy scree. It is one of the earliest, opening when the crocuses are in bloom elsewhere in the lawn. A berm or a garden raised with a wall is the best way to enjoy such small jewels.

round yellow "yolk" at the base inside. *T. clusiana*, a lipstick-red-striped white one with purple anthers, blooms in mid-May. This one is stoloniferous and will spread nicely! *T. praestans* 'Unicum' bears two to five bright red flowers per stem, with blue-black anthers and a small yellow base, on interesting, variegated leaves. Consult a good bulb catalog, which gives you the ability to choose a sample collection for your conditions, and after a season or two you'll know what will do best for you. Put these little bulbs where they are happy, and you will be charmed for years as they multiply.

Always Experimenting

I believe the gritty, well-drained berm may also be the best place for a new trial of *Cyclamen coum*, that miniature spring-blooming perennial bulb that is so wet-sensitive I have lost it to the wetness and exposure of a cold spring even after it has lived through a hard winter. I have always dreamed of having drifts of these tiny things, so like the bigger florist's plants, in pink, purple, and white with spotted leaves, though I know they are marginally hardy here. I would plant the bulbs in pockets of humusy soil nestled in the grit and see how that works. I am far less attracted to cyclamineums that bloom in autumn; they are so tiny, and given the browning perennial foliage and falling leaves that cover the ground in fall, I do not have a place where the little plants would be seen.

Full-Sized Tulips Too

I use hybrid tulips every year in my garden, but I never expect them to last more than a couple of years, so I replenish them regularly. They simply are not long-lasting, even using the best bulb fertilizer. It is too hard to give them the hot, dry summer baking they need, and besides, animals eat both bulbs and flowers. I like them best in large drifts of one color sweeping through parts of the borders and around shrubs, and I like to plan the colors to enhance other things growing and blooming at the same time.

It is critical to check the bloom times of your tulips if you wish to match them up with other plants. Good catalogs conveniently list tulips in order of flowering, though they may post somewhat earlier bloom times than we have in Zone 4. In the end, as with other things, a home trial is always the best way to establish bloom times. The later-blooming varieties are the best bets for accompanying our perennials, most of which do not bloom here until mid May. The lily-flowered varieties are especially stunning late accents when the garden is filling with foliage. Lily-flowering *Tulipa* 'Marriette', for instance, puts up its tall, elegant, pointed blooms of raspberry pink in late May for us, at the same time that *Epimedium x rubrum* shakes out its rosy clouds of starry flowers amidst olive foliage. What a duet.

An Outlandish Family of Bulbs

Fritillaries have always been favorites of mine. Their range is from modest and shy to bold and gaudy, so in effect they have something for everyone. I do not see them in many gardens, but I think that will change now that they are more available.

The common checkered lily, *Fritillaria meleagris*, is most familiar in its purple-and-cream checks. It has thin, stiff stems, about a foot tall, from which one or two of the two-inch bells hang exactly as if they should have clappers and ring in the breeze. Totally charming. They seed readily and are spreading nicely for me along a shaded slope. *F. m.* 'Alba' is pure white, 'Charon' is light purple with black checkering, and 'Saturnus' has bright reddish-purple flowers. I scatter the firm, round black seeds where I want new colonies to develop; they like a damp meadow, and some shade.

PHOTOGRAPH BY TOM COTTINGTON

PHOTOGRAPH BY TOM COTTINGTON

Top: *Fritillaria persica* forms a two-foot spire of purple bells, rising from a stem of up-pointing blue-green leaves, like a cross between a lily and a sedum in appearance. All of the fritillaries are exotic looking, and a large clump of these dark beauties will be a welcome addition as they spread slowly in the front garden.

Bottom: This charming fritilliary is a wildflower in England, where it is called checkered lily. Its proper name is *Fritillaria meleagris*. Success with this dainty thing depends on part shade and good, humusy soil, where it will seed around, producing an occasional white variant in its own natural way. I have had success with gathering the small black seeds when ripe and sewing them immediately in the right conditions, so that they appear by themselves in the spring.

Moving them is easy too: when you have a good bed prepared, get an ample trowelful of soil under the bulbs, and set them carefully where you want them. Since they have a tendency to seed right up next to the stems of daylilies and other bigger plants, this is a real blessing.

F. persica is a three-footer with long, glaucous, alternate leaves and tall spikes of bells, greenish-brown to deep purple. I have not grown the gaudier, big *F. imperialis*, mostly because it needs a dramatic setting of its own, and, like *F. persica*, it needs full sun and excellent drainage, especially over winter. The stiff, leafy stems of imperialis bear bright orange, red, or yellow pendant blooms, with a spiky crown of upright green leaves, in late spring. Perhaps in a new gritty berm, someday, I will feature these fritillaries and a few others I would really like to try as background for my smaller alpines. I recommend that you search for more of these bulbs and experiment with them. Even the shy little *F. meleagris* is a marvel to most visitors.

And Then the Lilies

Summer is never complete for me without the tall lilies. They are such good things to insert into any garden because they do not have huge, smothering bushes of leaves that crowd other plants, but rise on slender stalks to blossom in the air. *Lilium aurelian*, 'Black Dragon', 'Pink Perfection', or 'Golden Splendor', for example, add stunning height and color to any planting. All they need is good drainage and a mostly sunny location, though they will take up to half-shade if the sky is fairly open. The oriental lilies, sturdier and more upward- or outward-facing, are probably even more tolerant of conditions and bloom after the others are finished. These are now available in many hybrids, from the giant white blooms of *L. orientalis* 'Casa Blanca' to the petite *L. o.* 'Strawberry Shortcake'. I use a somewhat more restrained white one, *L. o.* 'Sterling Silver', with my border plantings; they are about the same height as Siberian irises, daylilies, single peonies, and astilbes, and set any of them off admirably.

Then I like the more delicate species lilies best for placement at the edge of a woods—*L. tigrinum* and *L.*

canadense for orange-red flowers, and *L. martagon* in all its newly introduced colors and hybrids: white, peach, and pink through red to mahogany.

These very early lilies are all endlessly pleasing to me, as they are happy in a naturalized woodland, in quite a bit of shade. They are loveliest at the edge of a dark patch of woods, with their small, curled blossoms hung in airy space. And such lots of them! I have seen martagon stalks with at least thirty blooms. A patch of all-white martagons against a dark wooded setting is simple perfection.

The Remarkable Onion Family

I am fond of alliums too, especially *Allium caeruleaum*, which produces the most heavenly sky-blue, nearly two-inch globes of fairy flowers on two-foot stems in July, and of course *A. senescens* 'Glaucum', which I use in dry borders. *A. stenocephalum*, the drumstick allium, is tall and a dull red-purple. *A. moly* has dainty yellow lily bells. *A. christophii* has ten-inch starry heads on somewhat shorter stems, and *A. giganteum* has huge, dense purple balls on tall stalks, which form great exclamation points even in a garden of large plants, such as peonies. I grow common chives, too, both for color in the garden and to use in cooking. These dry nicely for winter bouquets if picked at their peak. Garlic chives are larger than these, and make a beautiful, tall bunch of white globes, but look out! You will have nothing but a bed of them if you let them go to seed. All the alliums seed around and spread, but they are easy to pull up. All of them cut well and look beautiful in bouquets. And the more you cut, the fewer are left to go to seed!

Fall-Blooming Bulbs

I have only recently discovered the fall-blooming crocuses and colchicums. These large, glossy bulbs need good

soil, perfect drainage, and anything from half-sun to full. From bulbs planted in the spring, I had thick clumps of colchicum and *Crocus speciosus* goblets in luminous lavenders and white, eight inches tall, rising straight from the ground. Many blossoms arise from each bulb. It was unbelievable how long the blooming period lasted in their first year; one blossom for several days, and buds opening around it day after day. The big, strappy leaves of colchicum are a factor to deal with in spring, but I am learning to disguise the yellowing foliage with other plants.

The leaves of *C. speciosus* are not quite so obvious as those of colchicums, but then the flowers are much smaller, too, and somewhat less plentiful. Still, they are beautiful and persistent, increasing each year, and very tolerant of our soil conditions. The big bulbs of either must be planted in August, the very day they are received from the grower. They will bloom the first year. I place my bulbs near plants that have good leaf density in spring, in order to cover the maturing bulb leaves. When planting them, though, it is a test of memory, to recall how far those companion leaves spread, how long they last, and how much they might obscure the fall bulb flowers. Carefully done, this kind of planting has the added bonus of framing the fall blooms with lush surroundings. One of the most beautiful effects in my entire garden came from planting colchicum near *Hosta* 'White Christmas'—the leaves of *Thalictrum* 'Kiusianum', *Dicentra eximea*, and various petite ferns and flat rocks helping to set the composition. The little scene stayed fresh and bright until true frost.

This short chapter offers limited treatment, indeed, of the subject, but I plead mercy on the grounds that all I'd hoped to do was introduce you to the use of bulbs and tempt you to go further into that wonderland.

The Water Garden

Another solution for a town garden is to use water to create a very different atmosphere.

Even the smallest pools can bring an extra dimension to the garden setting.

Being able to touch water, watch reflections, or sit in the shade of arching bamboos

(provided their roots are restricted) will blot out the bricks and mortar beyond by

concentrating the mind in a tiny oasis of green.

Beth Chatto, *The Green Tapestry*, Simon & Schuster, 1989

F EVER ONE PART of the garden needed its own special book, it is the water feature. In this you are fortunate; since such gardens have risen so in popularity there are dozens of good books to help you. I do not presume to offer expert advice here. You will find plenty of how-to pamphlets. But I do want to add a word or two. My reasons are twofold: one, I would like to tell you how much my pond and waterfall have added to the enjoyment of my garden, so that you will consider planning a water feature of your own, and two, I might be able to help you avoid some of the mistakes we made.

My pond is homemade, dug and planned by myself and an enthusiastic neighbor. It is about nine feet long and four feet wide at its widest, and thirty-six inches deep (for the fish), except for a shelf around the ends and one side, about a foot from the surface. We dug out the topsoil and tossed it uphill to make a garden above one long edge, then hauled the deeper clay off into the woods. We laid sand and newspapers on the bottom, put in the liner, and added the water. Fish do well all year round, either with a stock-tank heater or a small pump running all winter to keep ice from covering the pond.

Advice from Painful Experience

All in all, the pond was pretty successful in its original state, but I do have a few cautions. The first difficulty I encountered was in the leveling and placement of the edging stones: I definitely had not cut the edge properly! It has taken years of recutting the bank and moving stones to obtain a natural-looking, safe edge that hides the liner and does not tip the unwary visitor down into the water. Do find a set of directions before digging your own pond; these will tell you to use enough liner to lay under a course of wide, level edging stones, on a slant down from the pond's edge, and to bring the liner up at the back of these stones where it

can be hidden in your lawn, garden, or patio. Do cut shelves for water plants about a foot deep around some of the edges, but not along the one side best suited for viewing the pond.

My second caution is not to choose too small a pump. Choose one that has a large hose, an inch or two in diameter, and plenty of strength to power a waterfall or a waterspout. Even if you think you will not want such a feature, get the larger pump now; small hoses clog up, small filters have to be lifted every few days and rinsed out, and if neglected choke off and burn out pumps. Fish are not aerated enough in hot weather by a small pump; they lie listlessly near the surface, and are then easily taken by raccoons and opossums.

Another caution is about fish: dig the pond three feet deep if you want fish to live, and lay a long, flat terra cotta chimney-tile on the bottom. Fish will rest in there, near the bottom, in the shade, as long as you give them oxygen enough, and animals will not have access to them.

My main caution is about materials. It was only after a couple of years that we discovered we had chosen too thin a liner, and that dogs, raccoons, or opossums had gouged holes in the sides as they climbed out after chasing my fish. We had to drain the pond of a thousand gallons of water and put the fish in a holding tank. That was a ghastly job! Much worse than the original pond-making project. We first put in the correct weight of heavy lining, then had to rearrange the (very!) heavy stones and boulders to better hold their positions, and then of course I had to do over the entire garden area around the circumference.

It was then I decided I would make a small pond on the slope above, that would form the beginning of a nice little waterfall at one end. Not! I made insufficient provision for sealing off the edges of the waterfall stream, and the water seeped rather than fell, and trickled away beneath the beautiful shelves of rock I'd arranged. Besides, the little pump did

Opposite: The sound and sparkle of water is the heart of the garden. This pond has taken on the feel of a stream, its narrow shape extending the length of the waterfall recently installed. Early in the season, before the overhanging greenery takes over, it is at its brightest.

not have the puff to force enough recycled water up into the pondlet. I soon realized I was never going to get the desired effect on my own. I called in a professional I found at a garden expo.

Expert Advice

There are now many professional companies which will design new ponds and consult on existing ponds. My consultant suggested a surface skimmer and a much larger pump and hose, to keep the water clear as glass, and to give enough force for a long, curved waterfall. The skimmer prevents the formation of rotting materials that caused the thick sludge I had to muck out every spring; fallen leaves now float off and are trapped. At the upper end of the waterfall, a sunken biological filter is filled with sacks of volcanic rock, which acts as a filter. The new, larger hose fills the filter tub with water fast enough to create a rushing waterfall. A wide, clear stream now pours over flat shelves of rock, down a curved track, and into the pond. Birds and little animals come to drink and bathe, dragonflies sail back and forth, and I have even had visiting leopard frogs sit on the wet stones. My original dream, but better. Fortunately, the original good design and placement of the pond were adaptable to these changes.

My water garden is in high shade. I cannot flower waterlilies prolifically because of this, but I do grow beautiful water plants in pots submerged on the shelves along the sides or sitting on the chimney tile in which my fish hide from raccoons.

Pondside Gardens

Two of my favorite small gardens flank the front of the pond, and they feature some of the choicest and smallest of my plants. The most dainty hostas and epimediums are set off perfectly by the water, and by the rocks and plants rising at the back of the pond where large-leaved, tall plants and ferns form a dense, tropical-looking background.

The pond is definitely the main focus of my back garden. Absolutely. It brings all the elements together, giving the whole a purpose. The sound of the water, and the glitter and rush of the falls, change the whole atmosphere. The stone terrace along the front has grown mossy over the years and provides enough room for several people to stand comfortably together, or for a small table and chairs and a pitcher of lemonade for two.

Conclusion

T IS A TRAIT of true gardeners that we will read through any garden book (especially one with pictures) with our antennae out, sifting and winnowing for new ideas we can apply to our own versions of paradise. As a class, gardeners work harder than other people to wring every last bit of good from their reading material. I can prove this. Who else, I ask you, would go through the thickest pile of catalogs, dozens of them, from January to May every year, choosing, listing, deleting, comparing, and adding again, without tiring or becoming in the least bored?

Ergo, if you have read this far, I say you are a true gardener. As such, there is nothing better I can say to you than "Welcome to the club."

And being a true gardener, you will no doubt have found something in this book worth retaining, if only a shared viewpoint or two. At least you know you have found a friend. So now I can imagine your gardens, spread all over the Upper Midwest, with perhaps, somewhere in each, a small corner inspired by this book. What a good thought.

Glossary

aerate	To incorporate air (into soil) with materials or tools.
alpine	Plant native to high altitudes, usually dwarfed.
amendments	Ingredients added to soil to bring it up to good tilth.
annual	Plant that completes its growing cycle in one season.
apical growth	Uppermost growing point; leader.
arborize	To cause to grow in tree form; to cut back to main trunks.
bacteria	Microscopic one-celled organisms.
biennial	Plant that grows from seed for one season, then blooms and dies in the second.
biodegradable	Capable of being decomposed by bacteria or other organisms.
bract	Leaflike form on flowering portion of plants.
bulb	Underground fleshy-leaved storage organ.
candles	Upright growing tips of conifers.
cane	Rose stem or branch.
capping	Hardening crust on soil around plants.
chlorophyll	Green pigment necessary for photosynthesis.
chlorosis	Reduction or loss of green coloration caused by iron deficiency.
clay	Stiff, sticky earth composed of fine particles.
companion plant	Plant that has a salutary effect on its neighbor(s).
compost	To decompose garden and kitchen waste; material so made.
conifer	Any evergreen of a group usually bearing cones.
corm	Underground swollen stem base.
cultivar	Hybrid word formed from the words *cultivate* and *variety*; a plant variety produced by cultivation.
culture	Process required for successful growing of plants.
deadhead	To remove spent blooms; material thus removed.
debud	To remove buds from blooming stems.
deciduous	Shedding leaves annually.
decomposition	Bacterial digestion of organic material.
dormant	Literally, sleeping: inactive period of growth.
drip line	Outer edge of a plant's canopy of leaves.
drought	Continuous absence of rain; dry weather.
ecology	Branch of biology dealing with environmental issues.
ephemeral	Blooming in early spring, then disappearing.
evergreen	Staying green year-round.
fertile	In regard to soil, having all the components, both mineral and organic, for growing plants.
fertilizer	Chemical or natural substance added to soil to make it fertile.
gardener	Person whose life is made better through working with plants.
genus	Group of species having common characteristics.
germinate	To sprout, as from seed.
glaucous	Having bluish or white indumentum on part of a plant.
green manure	Fresh plant material spaded under to decompose naturally.
habit	Mode of growth.
hardy	Able to survive extreme conditions.
head back	To prune growing ends of branches in order to improve lateral growth.
herb	Plant with aromatic oils (popular garden terminology).
herbaceous	Dying back to crown in the winter and regrowing in the spring.
herbicide	Substance used to destroy growing plants.
hips	Seedpods of roses.
humus	Decomposed organic material used as a component in fertile soil.
hybrid	Offspring of two plants of different species or varieties.
indumentum	Covering of fine hairs on part of a plant.

invasive	Vigorous to the point of being disagreeable.	shrub	Woody plant smaller than a tree with branches close to the ground.
loam	Fertile soil composed of clay, sand, and humus in proportion.	species	Class of similar plants that can exchange genes.
microorganism	Microscopic living creature, bacteria, for example.	spit	Depth of one spade.
mildew	Fungus that forms a wooly white coating on plants.	stolon	Horizontal stem with roots and new plants along its length.
moraine	Area of glacial deposits.	stoloniferous	Spreading by stolons.
mulch	Protective layer of material placed over plant roots.	strata	Layers of sedimentary materials hardened into rock.
native	Indigenous to a restricted local area.	subsoil	Soil directly beneath topsoil and devoid of organic matter.
naturalize	To introduce into an uncultivated situation.	succulent	Plant having water storage capacity in its stems and leaves.
naturalized plant	Introduced plant that thrives in a new environment.	suckers	Shoots arising from below-ground roots.
nutrients	Elements known to be required for healthy growth.	systemic	Material taken directly into a plant system.
organic	Material of plant or animal origin; culture restricted to such material.	till	To prepare and cultivate soil for planting.
		tilth	Condition of tilled soil.
pea-sticks	Woody branches, cut and dried, used to prop up growing plants.	topsoil	Top layer of soil; soil containing organic matter.
pedicel	Stalklike structure; stem of a leaf or flower.	underplanting	Juxtaposing early-, midseason-, and late-blooming plants for continuous and compatible growth.
pendant	Hanging.		
perennial	Plant that persists three or more years from its roots.	understory	Area beneath tall trees.
		variegated	Having broken coloration in leaves.
pesticide	Substance used to destroy insects.	variety	Natural variation from parent plant (species).
pinch back	To remove tips of apical or lateral growth.	volunteer	Self-sown plant.
propagate	To breed specimens by natural processes from parent stock.	water sprout	Shoot arising vertically along branches.
		xeric	Characterized by dry conditions.
provenance	Place of origin or history.	zone	Area designated by the U.S. Department of Agriculture based on plant hardiness and climate.
prune	To cut back in any of several ways.		
rhizome	Underground rootlike stem bearing both roots and shoots.		
scape	Leafless stem on which buds and blossoms form.		
scree	Accumulation of small loose stones; mountain slope covered with this material.		
sessile	Attached directly at base without having a stem.		

Index

activity guides

Paddling Southern Wisconsin: 82 Great Trips
by Canoe & Kayak, *Mike Svob*

Paddling Northern Wisconsin: 82 Great Trips
by Canoe & Kayak, *Mike Svob*

Great Cross-Country Ski Trails: Wisconsin, Minnesota,
Michigan & Ontario, *Wm. Chad McGrath*

Great Minnesota Walks: 49 Strolls, Rambles, Hikes & Treks,
Wm. Chad McGrath

Great Wisconsin Walks: 45 Strolls, Rambles, Hikes & Treks,
Wm. Chad McGrath

Wisconsin Golf Getaways: A Guide to More Than
200 Golf Courses, *Jeff Mayers & Jerry Poling*

travel guides

Wisconsin Garden Guide, *Jerry Minnich*

Bountiful Wisconsin: 110 Favorite Recipes, *Terese Allen*

Foods That Made Wisconsin Famous: 150 Great Recipes,
Richard J. Baumann

Wisconsin Herb Cookbook,
Susanne Breckenridge & Marjorie Snyder

Wild Wisconsin Notebook, *Jim Buchholz*

home and garden

Barns of Wisconsin, *Jerry Apps*

Portrait of the Past: A Photographic Journey Through Wisconsin
1865-1920, *Howard Mead, Jill Dean, and Susan Smith*

Walking Tours of Wisconsin's Historic Towns,
Lucy Rhodes, Elizabeth McBride, and Anita Matcha

Wisconsin: The Story of the Badger State, *Norman K. Risjord*

historical guides

Sacred Sites of Wisconsin, *John-Brian & Teresa Paprock*

Historical Wisconsin Getaways: Touring The Badger State's Past,
Sharyn Alden

Great Minnesota Weekend Adventures, *Beth Gauper*

Tastes of Minnesota: A Food Lover's Tour, *Donna Tabbert Long*

Great Iowa Weekend Adventures, *Mike Whye*

Great Indiana Weekend Adventures, *Sally McKinney*

The Great Wisconsin Touring Book: 30 Spectacular Auto Trips,
Gary Knowles

Wisconsin's Historic Houses & Living History Museums,
Krista Finstad Hanson

for young people

ABC's of Wisconsin, *Dori Hillestad Butler and Alison Relyea*

W is for Wisconsin, *Dori Hillestad Butler and Eileen Dawson*

H is for Hoosier, *Dori Hillestad Butler and Eileen Dawson*

Wisconsin Portraits: 55 People Who Made a Difference,
Martin Hintz

other titles of interest

Haunted Wisconsin, *Michael Norman & Beth Scott*

Driftless Spirits: Ghosts of Southwest Wisconsin, *Dennis Boyer*

The W-Files: True Reports of Wisconsin's Unexplained
Phenomena, *Jay Rath*

The I-Files: True Reports of Unexplained Phenomena in
Illinois, *Jay Rath*

The M-Files: True Reports of Minnesota's Unexplained
Phenomena, *Jay Rath*

For a free catalog, phone, write, or e-mail us.

Trails Books
P.O. Box 317, Black Earth, WI 53515
(800) 236-8088 • e-mail: info@wistrails.com
www.trailsbooks.com